U.S. History
Grades 5–12

I0170591

U.S. History Crossword Puzzles

Grades 5–12

SETTLEMENT
CIVIL RIGHTS
PRESIDENTS
IMMIGRATION
AMERICAN REVOLUTION
WESTWARD EXPANSION
INVENTIONS
INDUSTRIALIZATION
LAW
CIVIL WAR
RECONSTRUCTION
COLONIZATION
TRANSPORTATION
GOVERNMENT

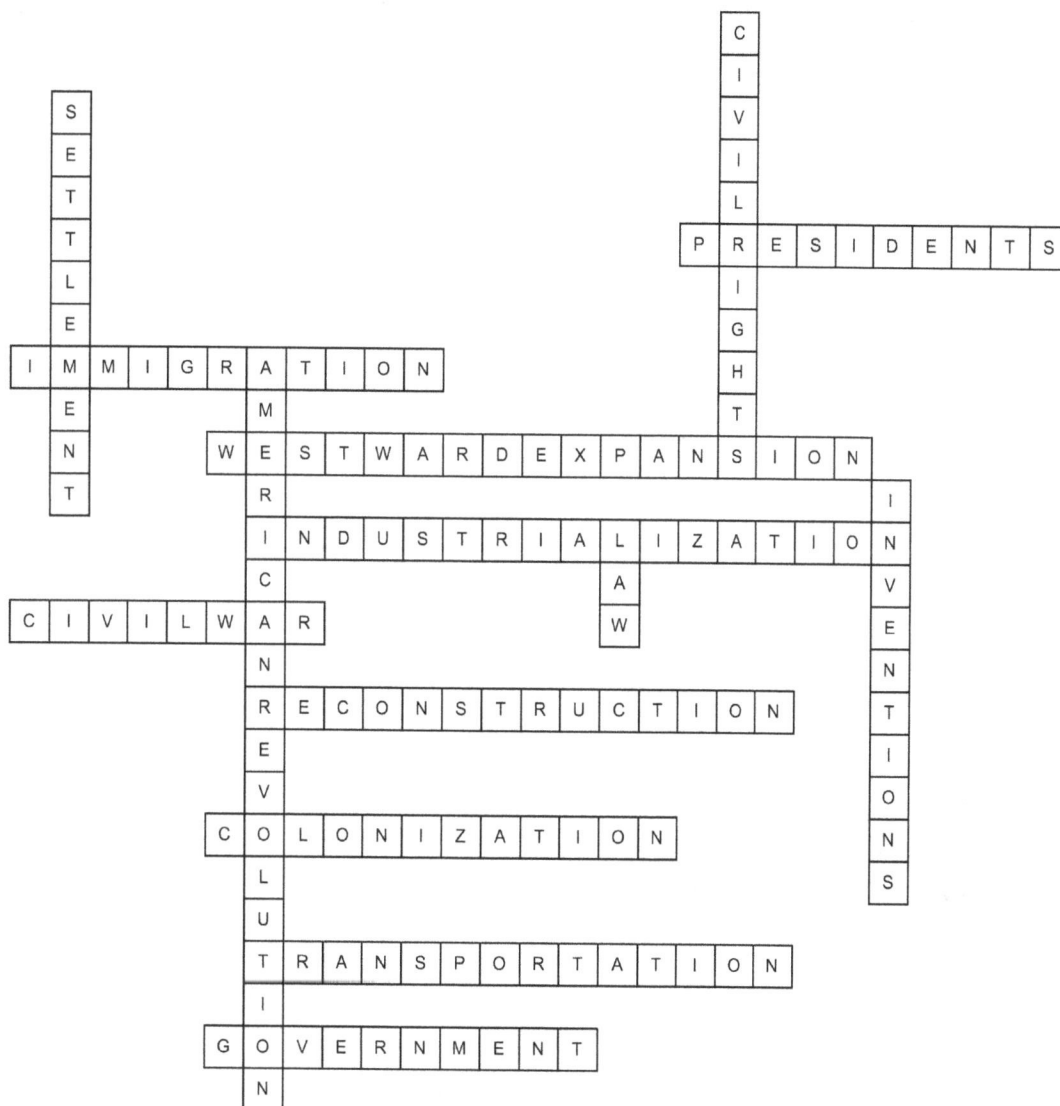

Written by Rebecca Stark

ISBN 978-1-56644-562-7

Educational Books 'n' Bingo

Printed in the United States of America.

TABLE OF CONTENTS

US HISTORY CROSSWORD PUZZLES **4–23**

Settlement and Colonization 4–5

The American Revolution 6–7

Westward Expansion 8–9

The American Civil War 10–11

Immigration 12–13

The Industrial Revolution 14–15

Presidents of the United States 16–17

Civics and Government 18–19

Civil Rights 20–21

U.S. History Potpourri 22–23

OTHER PUZZLES **24–26**

Commanders of the Civil War Word Search 24

Civil Rights Leaders Word Search 25

Hidden Cities 26

SOLUTIONS **27–40**

WORD LISTS FOR CROSSWORD PUZZLES* **41–42**

*An alphabetical list of answers from which to choose is provided for each crossword puzzle except the Presidents Puzzle; for that puzzle, a list of the Presidents in order of their presidency is provided. Use these lists at your discretion.

Settlement and Colonization

ACROSS

3. First permanent English settlement in the Americas; founded in Colony of Virginia in 1607
4. Came to New World for religious freedom; some founded Plymouth Colony in 1620
5. His daughter Pocahontas married John Rolfe
6. First agreement for self-government ever enacted in America (2 words)
7. Southern Colony established by James Oglethorpe
8. Florida city said to be oldest city in the United States (2 words)
9. Number of colonies that formed the United States of America
10. Puritans who settled in Plymouth Colony in what is now Massachusetts
12. Economic philosophy that pushed European nations to acquire as many colonies as possible
14. Made governor of New Netherlands in 1647
15. Founder of the British colony of Rhode Island (2 words)
16. Type of servant bound by contract to work for employer for a fixed period
17. Cecilius Calvert, the second ___; founded Maryland as a refuge for Catholics (2 words)
18. Produced for their commercial value; e.g., cotton, tobacco and rice in Southern Colonies (2 words)
19. Delaware, New Jersey, New York, and Pennsylvania; called the Breadbasket Colonies (2 words)
20. Chartered by James I in 1606 to establish settlements on the coast of North America (2 words)
23. City in Massachusetts known for witch trials
24. Canadian city founded by French explorer Samuel Champlain in 1608

DOWN

1. First grown in Colonies by John Rolfe of Jamestown
2. Fishing and shipping were important industries in the Northern, or ___ Colonies (2 words)
4. Large, cash-crop farm
6. Largest and most successful New England settlement; includes what is now Boston (3 words)
11. Postmaster and inventor; organized first trained volunteer fire department in America
21. Settled by Sir Walter Raleigh, this colony's inhabitants mysteriously disappeared
22. Founded by Puritans in 1620

Settlement and Colonization

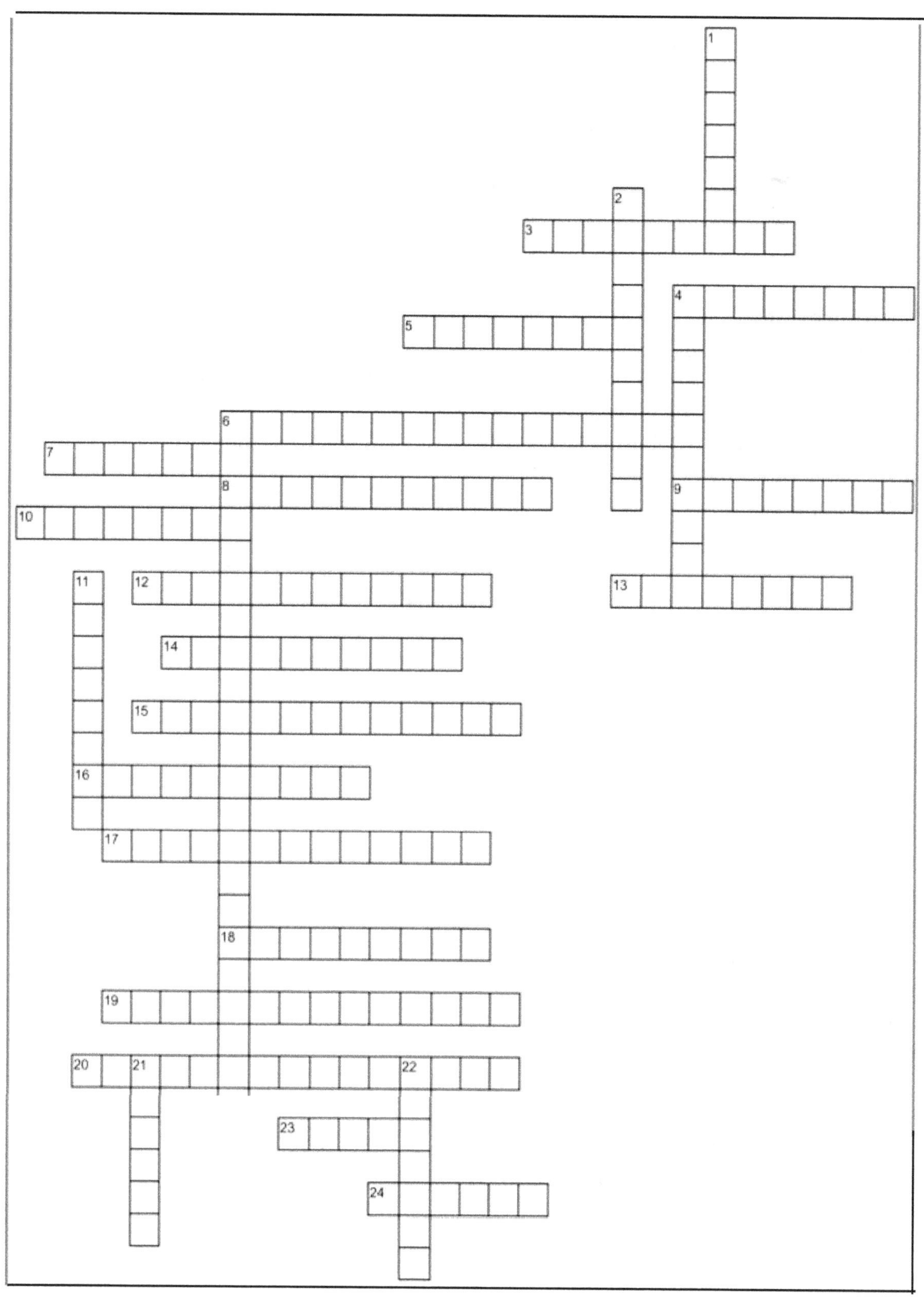

The American Revolution

ACROSS

1. Methods of guerrilla warfare earned him nickname of the "Swamp Fox"
6. Hanged in New York for spying against British troops
8. Postmaster General under the Continental Congress
10. Battle fought June 17, 1775, during siege of Boston (2 words)
12. Set up Committees of Correspondence to coordinate action against Great Britain (3 words)
15. First Vice President and second President of the United States (2 words)
16. Second Continental Congress adopted the Declaration of ___
19. Liberty Bell is located in this city
20. German auxiliaries who fought for Great Britain
22. French soldier who helped the American cause
25. Led the Continental Army to victory; first President of the United States
26. This New York battle considered turning point in the wa
27. American woman said to have fought in Battle of Monmouth (2 words/nickname)
29. Leader of Green Mountain Boys
30. The ___ Acts were passed to punish Massachusetts for the Boston Tea Party
32. Member of Sons of Liberty; called "Father of the American Revolution" (2 words)
33. The ___ Act of 1774 said soldiers could be housed in occupied private homes
35. Ruling monarch of Great Britain during American Revolution: ___ III (2 words)
36. Battle of ___ , Virginia; last major battle of the war
37. Colonists objected to ___ without representation

DOWN

1. Fought British regulars at Lexington and Concord
2. Polish soldier who became a general in the Continental Army
3. Leader of the Kentucky militia
4. He and Dawes warned Hancock & S. Adams of movements of the British
5. Colonists who sided with Great Britain; "Loyalists"
7. Continental Army camped here during harsh winter of 1777–1778 (2 words)
9. "Financier of the Revolution"
10. Crispus Attucks was killed as a result (2 words)
11. Known for pamphlet "Common Sense"
13. Prime Minister of Great Britain 1770 to 1782
14. He said, "Give Me Liberty or Give Me Death!"
17. His 1781 defeat at Yorktown, Virginia, considered end of the war
18. First to sign the Declaration of Independence
21. The ___ Act of 1765 was first direct tax imposed on the colonies
23. Union General turned traitor
24. The Green Mountain Boys captured this fort
28. Principal author of the Declaration of Independence
31. Treaty of ___ formally ended the United States of America's War for Independence
34. "Father of the American Navy"

The American Revolution

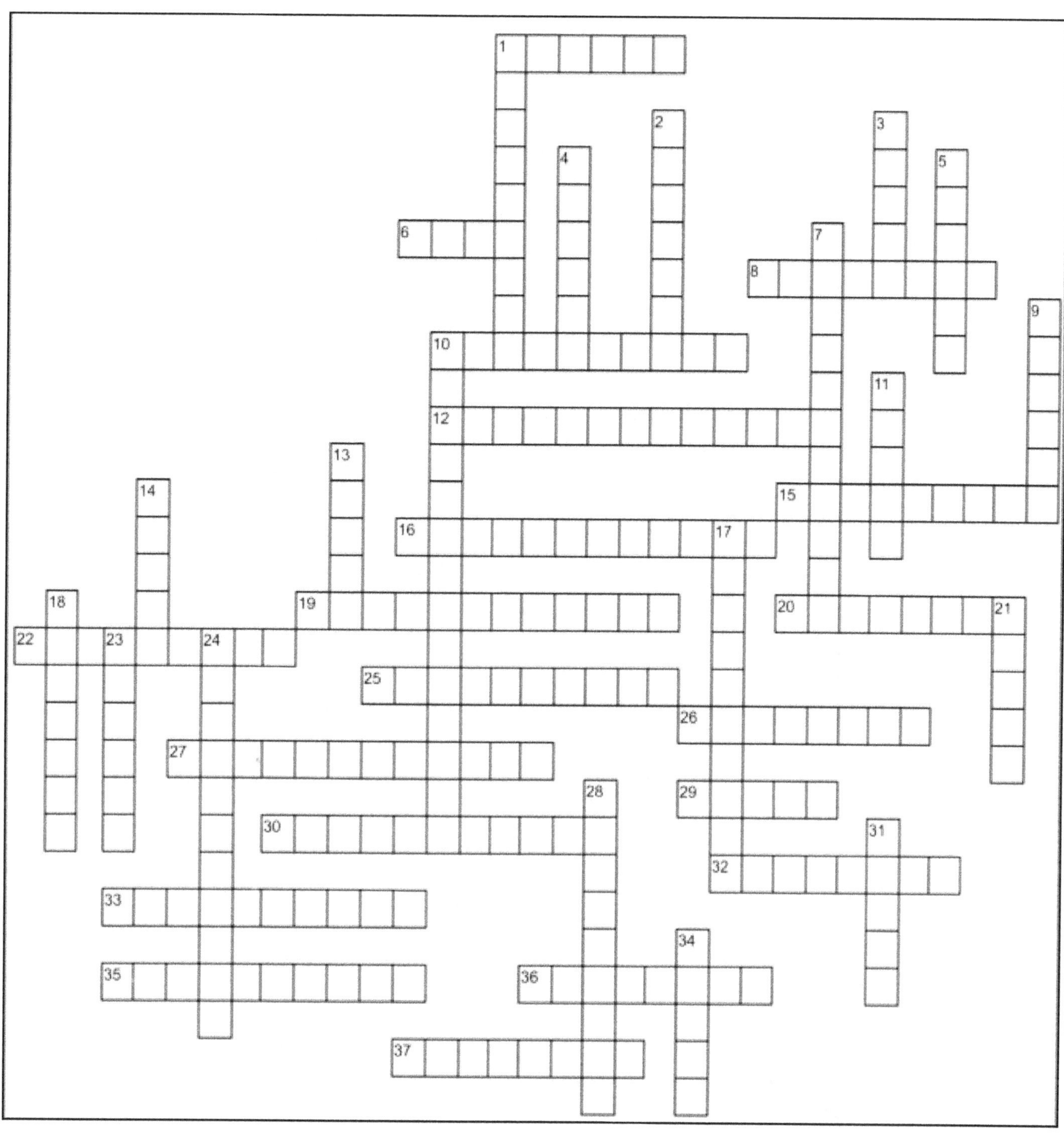

Westward Expansion

ACROSS

2. Co-captain of Corps of Discovery
4. Enabled people and goods to move to and from West; for example, the Erie, Chesapeake, and Ohio
5. Led Core of Discovery expedition to explore Louisiana Territory
7. Influential journalist; founded *New York Tribune* in 1841; advocate of the westward movement
8. President when Congress passed the Indian Removal Act
10. It warned European countries to stop colonization in the Western Hemisphere (2 words)
11. Under his leadership the Mormons organized the Utah Territory (2 words)
12. Treaty that added southern Arizona and southwestern New Mexico to US (2 words)
13. Belief that expansion of the United States across North America was inevitable (2 words)
14. Shawnee chief, warrior, statesman, and orator; on British side in War of 1812
16. Break in Appalachian Mountains located by Daniel Boone (2 words)
18. Went from Cumberland, Maryland, to Wheeling, Virginia (2 words)
22. Used to describe Indian Removal that occurred from 1830 to 1850 (3 words)

DOWN

1. Frontiersman who blazed trail known as the Wilderness Road through the Cumberland Gap (2 words)
3. Ordinances of 1785 and 1787 established how this territory would be divided and governed
4. Leader of Nez Perce; in surrender speech said, "I will fight no more forever" (2 words)
6. Shelter popular in the wilderness areas of Pennsylvania, Kentucky, Tennessee, and Ohio (2 words)
9. 1803 transaction between France and the United States that greatly enlarged size of the United States (2 words)
15. Called the "Gateway to the West"; edge of the United States frontier near confluence of the Missouri and Mississippi rivers (2 words)
17. Highest summit of the southern Front Range of the Rocky Mountains; named for leader of first American expedition that tried to climb it (2 words)
19. Explored new regions of US; drew and painted the unique plants and animals he encountered
20. Territory that became the resettlement site for displaced Native Americans of the Southeast
21. Act that gave 160 acres to anyone willing to live on it for five years
23. Baltimore and Ohio was first common carrier ___; founded in 1828
24. The Oregon, Santa Fe, California, Old Spanish, and Mormon were Important overland ___
25. Defeat at battle at this mission became rallying cry for Texas' Independence from Mexico
26. Shoshone woman who was helpful to Lewis and Clark

Westward Expansion

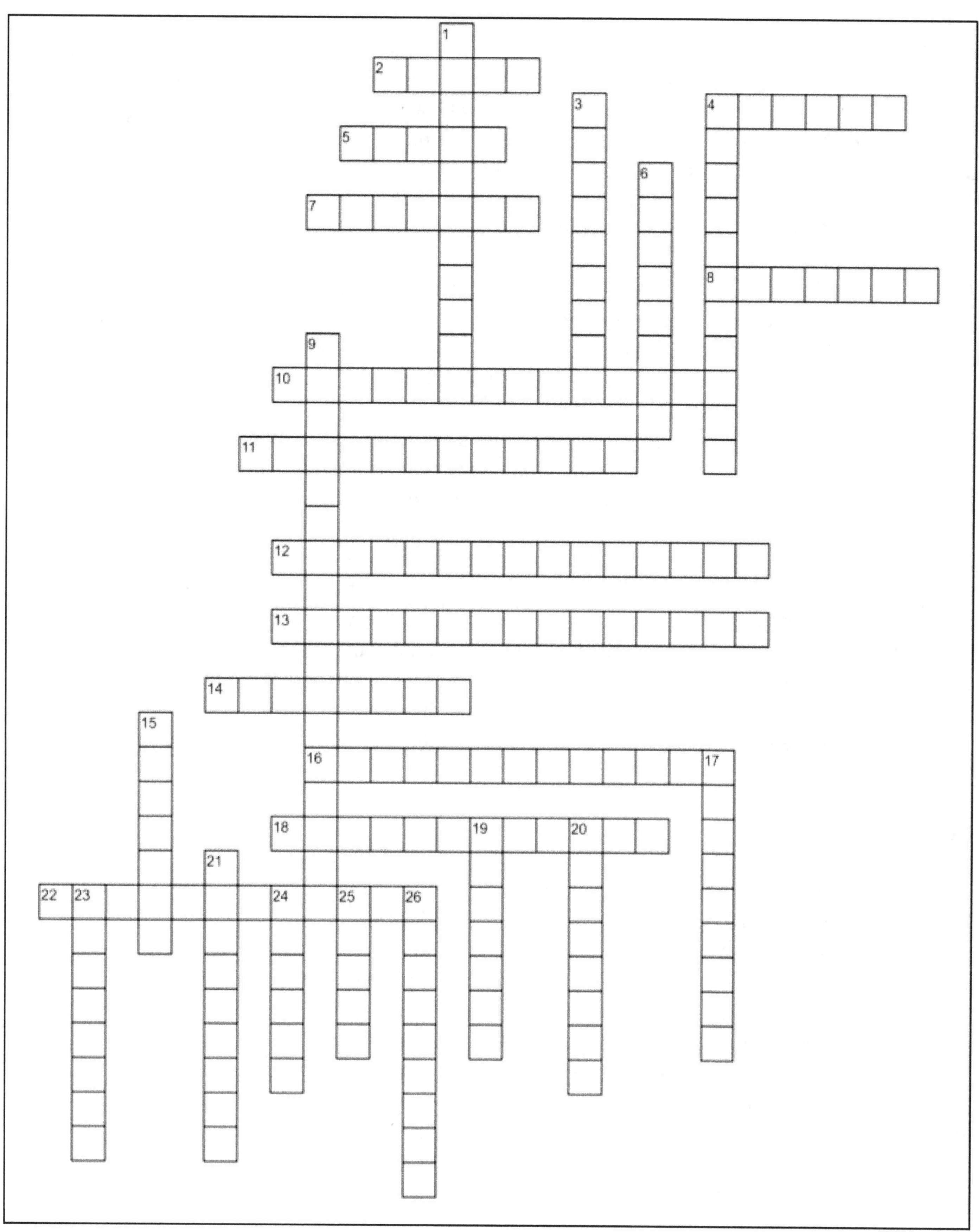

The American Civil War

ACROSS

4. Victory here gave Union control of the entire Mississippi River and split Confederacy in half
6. Name used to signify the North during the American Civil War
7. First battle here was the first major land battle of the war (2 words)
8. Commander-in-Chief of the Confederate Armies
9. Made Commander-in-Chief of the Federal armies in 1864
11. President of the Confederate States of America (2 words)
14. President of the United States during the American Civil War (2 words)
15. Hanged for trying to get enslaved African Americans in Harpers Ferry, VA, to rebel (2 words)
16. Lee's May 3, 1863, victory here considered his greatest victory
17. Three-day battle in PA; bloodiest battle of the war with 51,000 casualties
19. One who supported the movement to make slavery illegal
20. Nickname of General John C. Frémont
21. Large farms that dominated southern agriculture from the mid-18 century to the Civil War
23. Assertion that states can ignore federal laws; eventually led to secession
24. Period after Civil War when federal government focused on resolving problems brought about by the war
25. What Southerners called Northerners who moved to the South during Reconstruction
27. Founder of the American Red Cross; organized relief for wounded soldiers (2 words)
28. The South favored ___; the North wanted the federal government to have more power (2 words)
29. Sided with the Union; Delaware, Kentucky, Maryland, Missouri, and West Virginia (2 words)
33. Imposed by Union to prevent supplies, troops, or other aid from reaching South
34. Union general best known for his destruction of the Shenandoah Valley
35. Union victorious at this major battle in Western Theater; also known as the Battle of Pittsburgh Landing

DOWN

1. Where first engagement of the American Civil War took place (2 words)
2. Term for withdrawing from a political entity
3. Battle of *CSS Virginia* (AKA the *Merrimack*) vs. the *USS Monitor* was first battle between ___
5. Southern city captured by General Sherman and his troops in September 1864
10. His "March to the Sea" ended with the capture of Savannah on December 22, 1864
12. Document that freed all slaves in the Confederate States (2 words)
13. Formed by the 11 southern states that seceded from the Union
18. Nineteenth-century photographer; best known for documentation of American Civil War
22. Battle in Maryland won by Union; bloodiest one-day battle in American history
26. Nickname given to General Jackson at First Battle of Bull Run (2 words)
30. Amendment to the Constitution that ended slavery in the United States
31. Taxes paid on goods from foreign countries; Southerners thought they were unfair
32. What General Lee did at Appomattox Court House, Virginia

The American Civil War

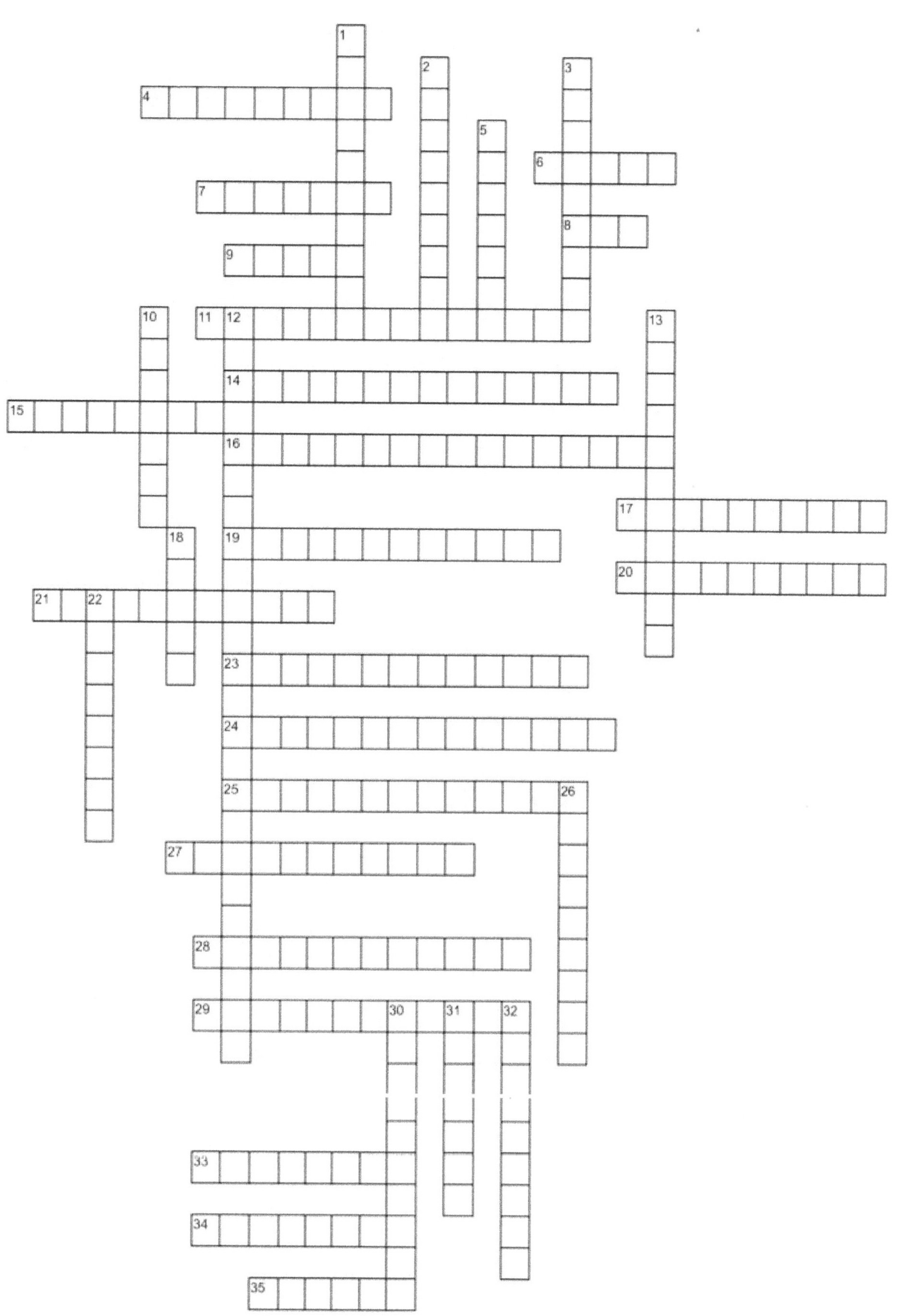

Immigration

ACROSS

9. Eventually became the largest single group of European immigrants
10. The first significant federal legislation restricting immigration; passed in 1882 (3 words)
13. Busiest immigrant inspection station in U.S.; from 1892–1954 processed about 12 million immigrants (2 words)
15. Colossal sculpture in New York Harbor given to the people of the United States by the French
16. Immigration Act of 1917 was first federal law to use a ___ to restrict immigration (2 words)
17. American labor union leader
19. Senator who in 1896 proposed a bill that would limit the entry of immigrants (3 words)
20. Most immigrants from 1815 to 1865 came from hailed from Northern and Western ___
22. Encouraged Western migration by providing settlers 160 acres of public land (2 words)
23. System limiting number of immigrants who may enter the United States each year by nationality; Immigration and Nationality Act of 1965 did away with this system
24. Person is an ___ upon leaving homeland and an immigrant upon arriving at new country
26. America's first official immigration center; closed due to allegations of abusive behavior toward immigrants (2 words)
27. This event caused many Irish to immigrate to America (2 words)
30. ___ from Eastern Europe fled religious persecution, especially the Russian pogroms
31. Most passengers on the steamships chose this cheapest rate

DOWN

1. Her poem is inscribed on pedestal on which the Statue of Liberty stands (2 words)
2. Also known as the Immigration Act of 1924, this act created quota system favoring immigrants from Western Europe and prohibiting those from Asia (hyphenated word)
3. Many Europeans who made the costly voyage became this type of servant
4. Political party that opposed immigrants and Catholics; prominent during late 1840s and early 1850s (hyphenated word)
5. Many Asian immigrants settled in California as part of the ___, which began with the discovery at Sutter's Mill (2 words)
6. To acquire the social and psychological characteristics of the dominant culture of a society
7. Action of coming to live permanently in a foreign country
8. Immigrants had to pass through ___ at the pier before entering the United States
11. Period during which agrarian, rural societies became industrial and urban (2 words)
12. Those from Asia generally entered through customs facilities on the ___ (2 words)
14. Most European immigrants came to the United States by crossing the Atlantic Ocean on one
18. More than 70 percent of all immigrants entered through this city, which came to be known as the "Golden Door" (2 words)
21. Immigrants from Europe generally came through ___ facilities (2 words)
25. She created Hull House in Chicago, which provided immigrants with education and training (2 words)
28. Many immigrants who worked in cities lived in these crowded, rundown apartment houses
29. A person who comes to one country from another to settle

Immigration

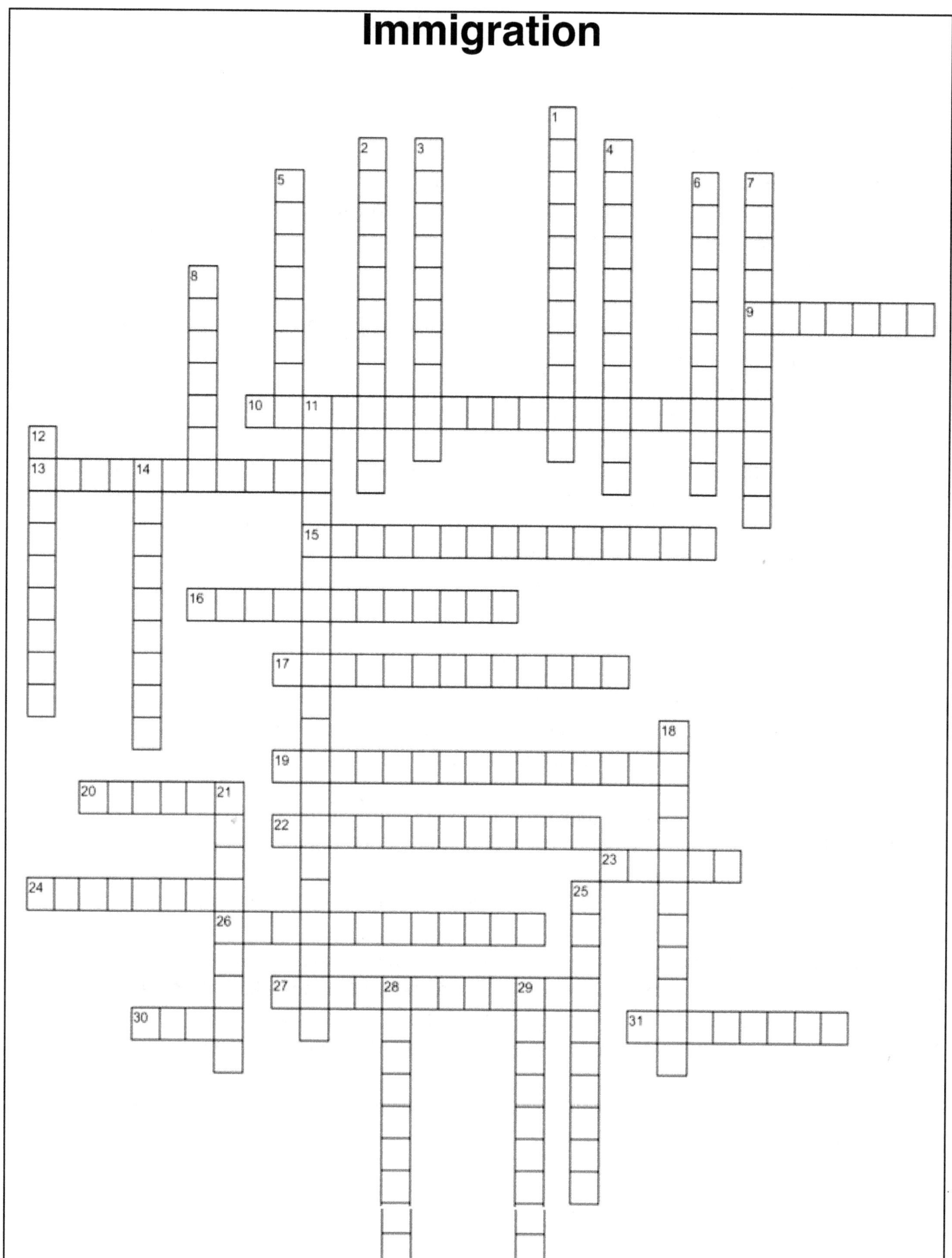

The Industrial Revolution

ACROSS

4. Technological changes included the use of these new basic materials: ___ and iron
7. Eventually held 1,093 patents on his inventions
8. Developed an electric telegraph and a code using electrical pulses of varied lengths
10. Situation when person or group has complete control over all aspects of a specific market
11. Small scale industries in people's homes; replaced by factories in Industrial Age (2 words)
13. A fire in the ___ Factory in New York City caused death of 146 factory workers (2 words)
14. Development of industries in a country or region on a wide scale
16. Applying specialization, division of labor, and standardization of parts to produce large amounts of goods in a less costly, more efficient manner (2 words)
17. He set out to get complete control of the oil industry
18. The vast influx of ___ between 1800 and 1900 provided the new industrial cities of the East with inexpensive labor
22. Clustering and concentration of large numbers of people into a relatively small area, resulting in cities
24. During the Industrial Revolution, shrewd businessmen created monopolies to avoid this
25. The means employed to provide objects necessary for human sustenance and comfort
26. He developed and improved agricultural tools
27. Best known for his invention of the cotton gin

DOWN

1. Creating and introducing something new
2. Social reformer concerned about the growing problems of the city poor (2 words)
3. Became common because they worked for low wages and fit into small places (2 words)
4. Many factories were called this because of the bad working conditions
5. Through industrialization, labor became ___
6. Built to provide workers with affordable housing close to the factories
9. The Baltimore and Ohio ___ was the first one chartered in the United States
11. Most powerful businessmen of the era were called this (3 words)
12. Largest city of American Midwest; its location made it valuable for moving freight between the coasts
15. Founded as fur-trading post; became transportation hub as result of steamboat era
19. Credited with creating the modern, integrated, mass-production operation (2 words)
20. Buildings where goods are manufactured or assembled chiefly by machine (2 words)
21. Andrew Carnegie, Thomas Mellon, and other Industrial giants built steel empires there because of availability of raw materials
23. Irish-American given credit for being the first to successfully install a steam engine as the power source on a boat

The Industrial Revolution

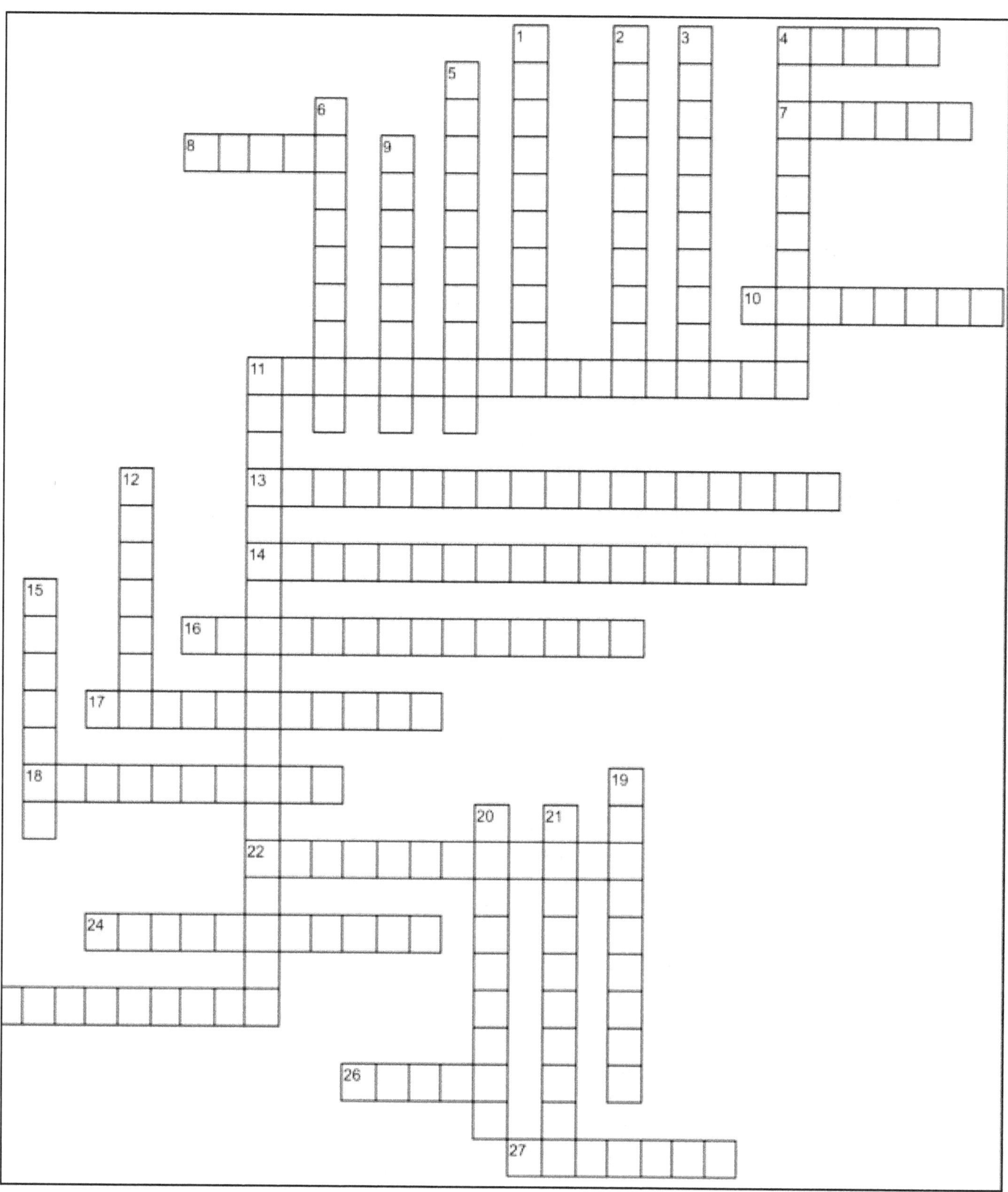

Presidents of the United States

NOTE: Use only last names unless otherwise instructed. A list of the Presidents and their dates served is provided on page 42.

ACROSS

2. Created the Department of Energy and the Department of Education
5. First African-American President of the United States; in office when Affordable Care Act was enacted
6. Gadsden Purchase, signed during his presidency, brought parts of present-day Arizona and New Mexico into U.S.
9. Signed the Immigration Act of 1924, which limited the number of immigrants who could be admitted to the U.S.
11. Resigned from office because of the Watergate Scandal
13. Appointed Daniel Webster Secretary of State
16. Bill of Rights was adopted during his presidency
18. Bribery incident known as Teapot Dome Scandal took place during his administration
20. Son of 2nd President. Wrote the Monroe Doctrine while Secretary of State (full name, 3 words)
22. President at the time of the Louisiana Purchase
23. First to succeed a resigning President; pardoned Richard Nixon upon taking office
24. Sometimes called the "Father of Civil Service"
26. President during Persian Gulf War, code-named Operation Desert Storm (first and last names and 2 middle initials)
28. Alien and Sedition Acts passed during his Presidency
29. Only President to be elected for four terms
30. Was General in Chief of all Federal Armies during the American Civil War
31. In office when World Trade Center in New York was attacked (first and last names and middle initials)
33. Was commanding general of the victorious Allied forces in Europe during World War II
35. Was governor of Arkansas before becoming President
36. Ordered atomic bombs to be dropped on Hiroshima and Nagasaki in August 1945
37. Issued the Emancipation Proclamation in 1862
39. War of 1812 took place during his presidency

DOWN

1. First president not born a British subject
3. Civil Rights Act of 1964 was passed during his administration (last name)
4. The Spanish-American War took place during his administration
7. The 19th Amendment, which granted women the right to vote, was passed during his administration
8. Iran-Contra Affair, involving trading arms for hostages, took place during his administration
9. Only President to serve two nonconsecutive terms
10. President during the Mexican-American War
12. His doctrine declared opposition to European intervention in the Americas
14. Confederate States of America formed while he was President, but Civil War didn't take place while in office
15. His Square Deal included conservation of natural resources & control of corporations (first and last name)
17. Became President when William Henry Harrison died after only one month in office
18. Great Depression began in 1929 during his administration with the crash of the New York Stock Market
19. Shot on July 2, 1881, by Charles Guiteau; died a few months later
21. During the 13-day Cuban Missile Crisis took place during his presidency
22. Indian Removal Act was passed during his presidency
25. Real-estate tycoon and reality-tv star; presidency his first elected office
27. Political opponents called him "His Fraudulency" as a result of the Compromise of 1877
32. Nicknamed "Old Rough and Ready"; hero of Mexican-American War
34. Sherman Anti-Trust Act, the first federal act to prevent monopolies, passed during his presidency
38. Became Chief Justice of the United States after being President

Presidents of the United States

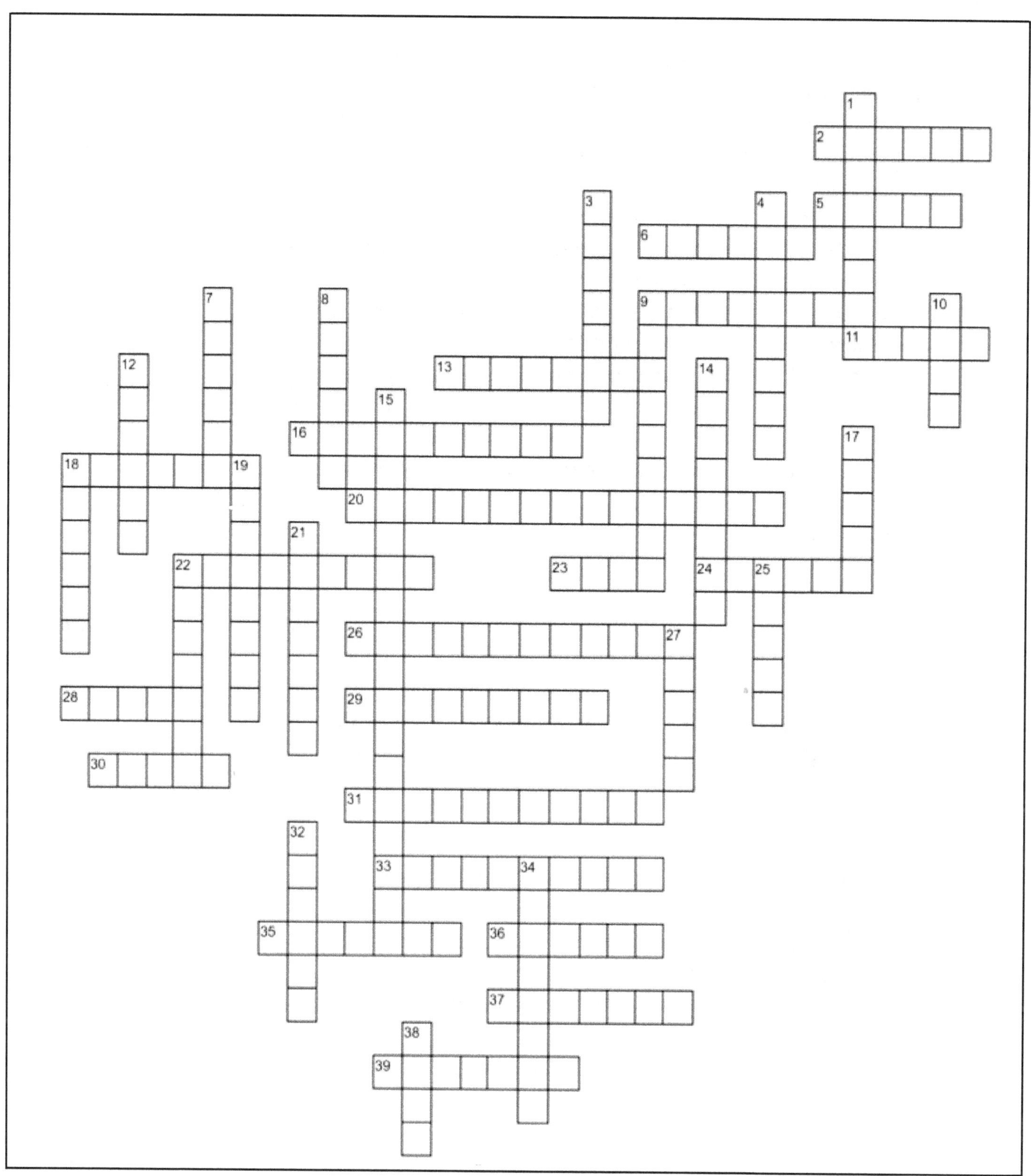

Civics and Government

ACROSS

1. This body can initiate spending bills and has exclusive authority to impeach officials (shortened form)
4. Formal indication of a choice between two or more candidates or courses of action
7. Highest federal court of the United States (2 words)
8. To give a group of people the right to vote
9. Focuses on overseas intelligence gathering (acronym)
12. Branch of government that makes the laws; made up of the two houses of Congress
13. The first 10 amendments to the U.S. Constitution
14. A person can be elected President for ___ terms, but can serve as many as ten years
16. A formal charge or accusation of a serious crime
20. Official residence and workplace of the President of the United States (2 words)
22. Fundamental law of the United States; drafted in Philadelphia in 1787
24. Form of government in which the greatest power is vested in the people
25. An action, such as a prolonged speech, that obstructs progress in a legislative assembly
27. ___ comprises the Senate and the House of Representatives
28. What a bill becomes once it is signed by the President or his veto is overridden by both houses
29. A draft of a law presented to a legislature for enactment
30. To charge the holder of a public office with misconduct

DOWN

2. Branch of U.S. government headed by President; responsible for seeing laws of the land are enforced
3. The19th amendment to the Constitution granted women this
5. The top leaders of the executive branch
6. Power of a President or governor to reject a bill proposed by a legislature
7. Presides over the United States House of Representatives (4 words)
10. Only the ___ can approve treaties
11. Domestic intelligence and security service of the United States; principal federal law enforcement agency (acronym)
15. Headquarters of the United States Department of Defense
17. When you vote for President, you are actually voting for the candidate's ___
18. Used to refer to the central government of the United States
19. An article added to the United States Constitution
21. Branch made up of judges appointed by the president and confirmed by the Senate
23. To give evidence as a witness in a law court
26. Our system of checks and ___ gives specific powers to the 3 branches of government
27. Study of the rights and duties of citizenship

Civics and Government

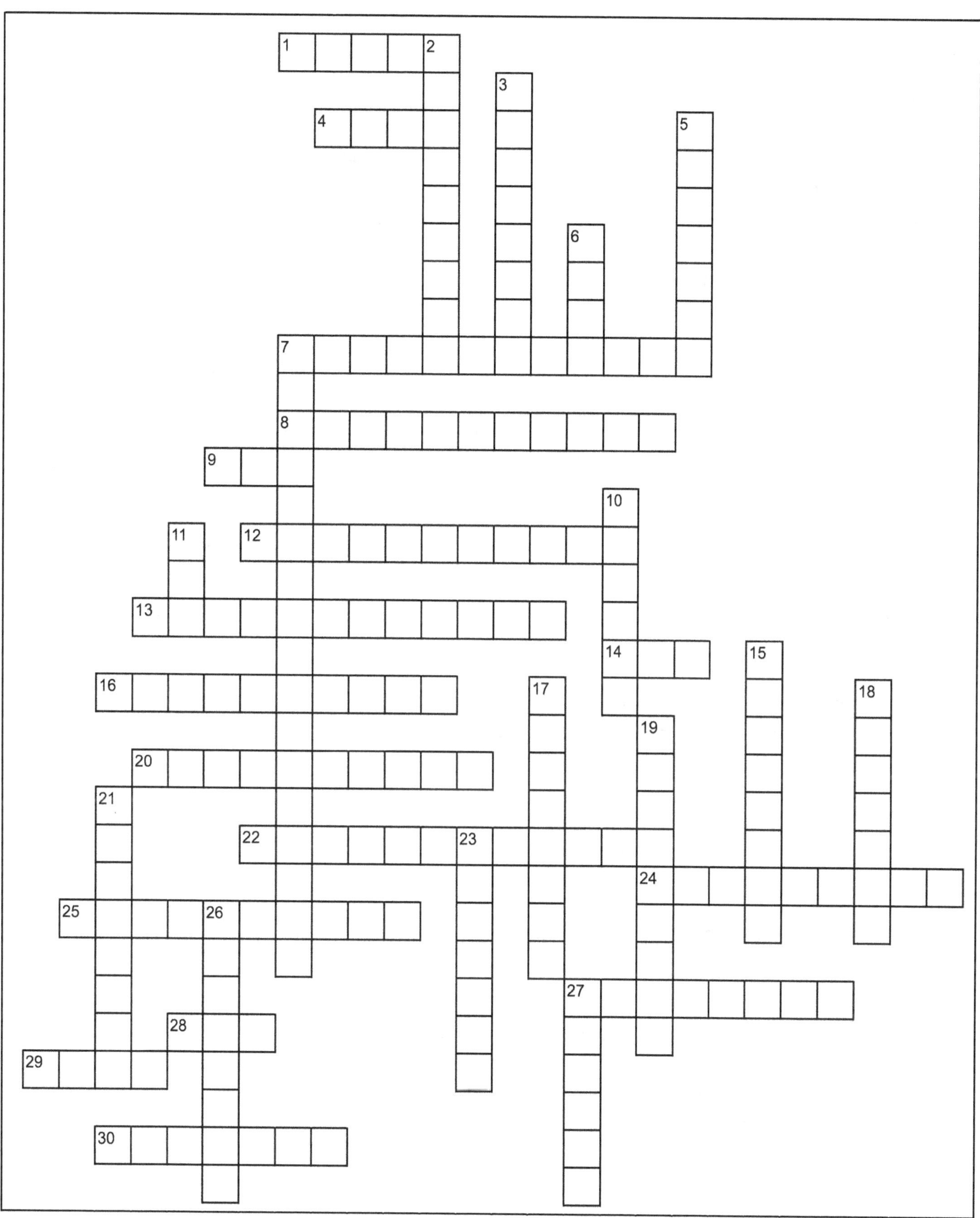

Civil Rights

NOTE: The list of possible answers on page 42 shows people's full names; however, you should follow the specific instructions given in parentheses after the clues.

ACROSS

3. Acronym for National Association for the Advancement of Colored People; a civil rights organization
6. Made his "I Have a Dream" speech during the March on Washington for Jobs and Freedom on August 28, 1963 (last name)
7. First lady who was outspoken in behalf of civil rights causes (first and last names)
9. Most famous "conductor" on the Underground Railroad (first and last names)
10. The 13th, 14th and 15th amendments to the Constitution are called the ___ Amendments
12. One of the founders of the NAACP; she documented lynching in the United States (last name)
15. Author of *Go Tell It on the Mountain* (first and last names)
16. Amendment that said the right of citizens to vote shall not be denied or abridged on account of race, color, or previous condition of servitude
17. Co-founder of the Leadership Conference on Civil Rights; leader of NAACP (first and last names)
18. Town in New York State where first women's rights convention was held in 1848 (2 words)
21. Born a slave, he was an abolitionist, author and orator (first and last names)
23. Women's rights activist and abolitionist (first and last names)
24. First openly gay person to be elected to public office in California; civil and human rights leader; murdered in 1978 (first and last names)
26. Amendment that said all persons born or naturalized in the United States are citizens

DOWN

1. President who signed the Civil Rights Act of 1964 was passed (last name)
2. First African American to earn a PhD from Harvard University in 1895; co-founder of NAACP (last name)
4. In 1916, formed the National Woman's Party; fought for passage of 19th amendment (first and last names)
5. Acronym for Congress of Racial Equality
7. Prohibited slavery in states in rebellion against the United States (2 words)
8. Amendment that abolished slavery in the United States
11. Laws that mandated the segregation of public schools, public places, public transportation, and other places (2 words)
13. National chairman of Congress of Racial Equality (last name)
14. Founded the League of Women Voters (last name)
19. Known for her refusal to surrender her bus seat to a white passenger (first and last names)
20. Co-founder of the Hull House and American Civil Liberties Union (first and last names)
22. Formed the National Women's Loyal League with Susan B. Anthony (last name)
25. Leader in women's suffrage movement (last name)
27. Civil rights activist; assassinated in 1963 outside of his home in Jackson, MS (last name)

Civil Rights

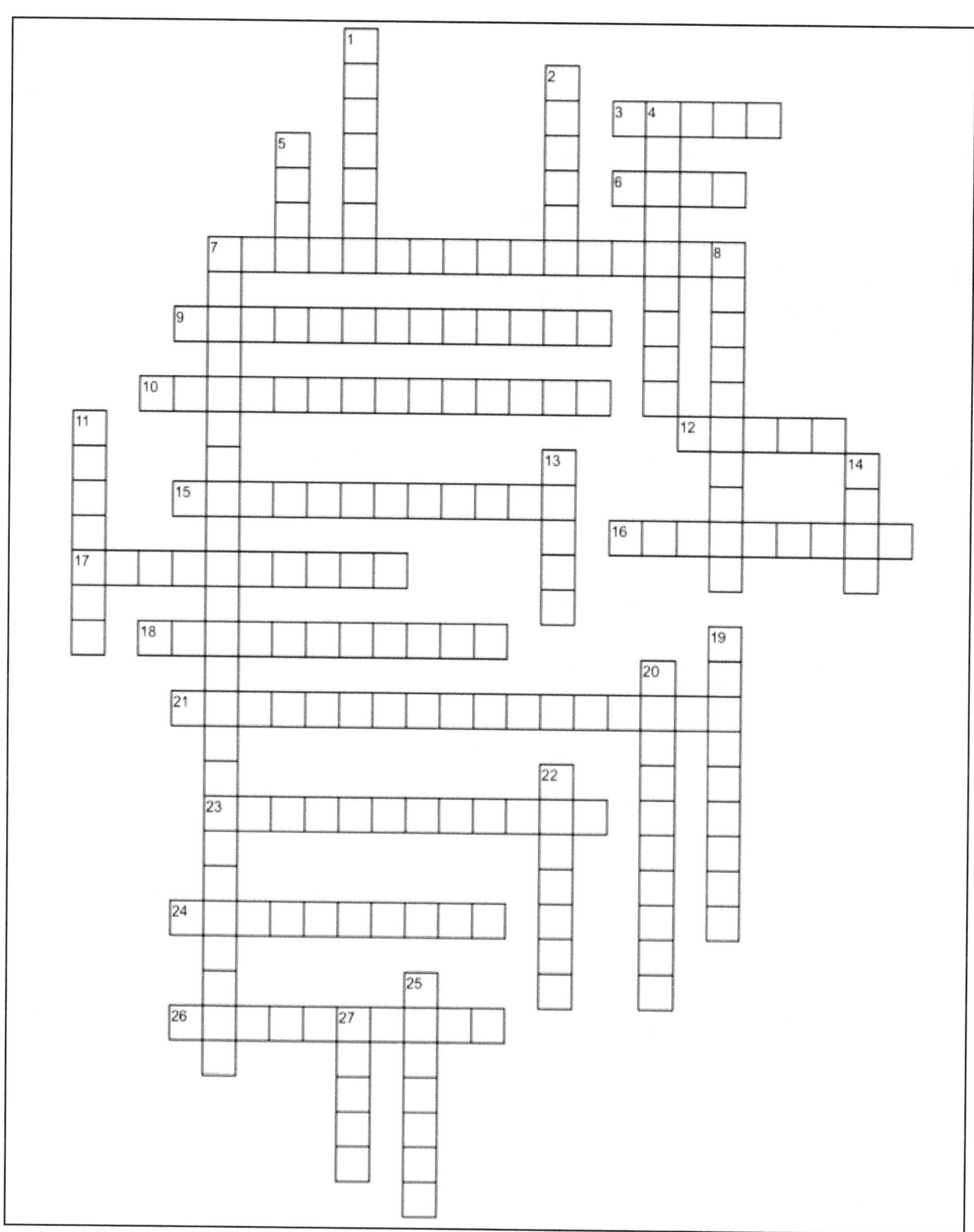

U.S. History Potpourri

ACROSS

3. Nicknamed the Swamp Fox because of guerrilla warfare tactics during American Revolution
5. Wrote pamphlet "Common Sense" to convince colonists to become independent from Britain religion, press, assembly, and petition
7. It began using horse-and-rider relay teams to shuttle mail along a 2,000-mile route In April 1860 (2 words)
8. First 10 amendments to the Constitution (3 words)
9. Forced removal of Native Americans under the Indian Removal Act of 1830 (3 words)
12. Battle here considered turning point of the American Revolution
13. Attacked by Japanese on December 7, 1941 (2 words)
15. Wars that were part of a larger war between Great Britain and France (3 words)
17. Discovery of ___ at Sutter's Mill in 1848 led about 300,000 people to go to California
18. Fought for women's suffrage
22. A protective one is a tax placed on goods from another country to protect the home industry
24. Many Americans lost their jobs and their money during the Great ___ of the 1930s
26. To approve by vote
28. First Battles of American Revolution: Lexington and ___

DOWN

1. Apollo 11 was first space mission to successfully land here
2. Amendment that protects freedom of speech, religion, press, assembly, and petition
3. Francis Scott Key wrote the "Star Spangled Banner" when flag was raised over this fort in 1814
4. Second President of the United States
6. Purchased from Napoleon during President Jefferson's administration in 1803 (2 words)
10. University that is oldest institution of higher learning in United States.
11. 50th State
14. First permanent English settlement in New World; founded 1606
16. Drought-stricken Southern Plains region of the United States in the 1930s (2 words)
19. Invented bifocals
20. His cotton gin speeded the cleaning of cotton fibers, increasing the desire for slaves
21. Address that began "Four score and seven years ago"
23. Known for his "Give me liberty or give me death" speech
25. Author of *Uncle Tom's Cabin*
27. His successful use of the steamboat revolutionized U.S. transportation and trade

U.S. History Potpourri

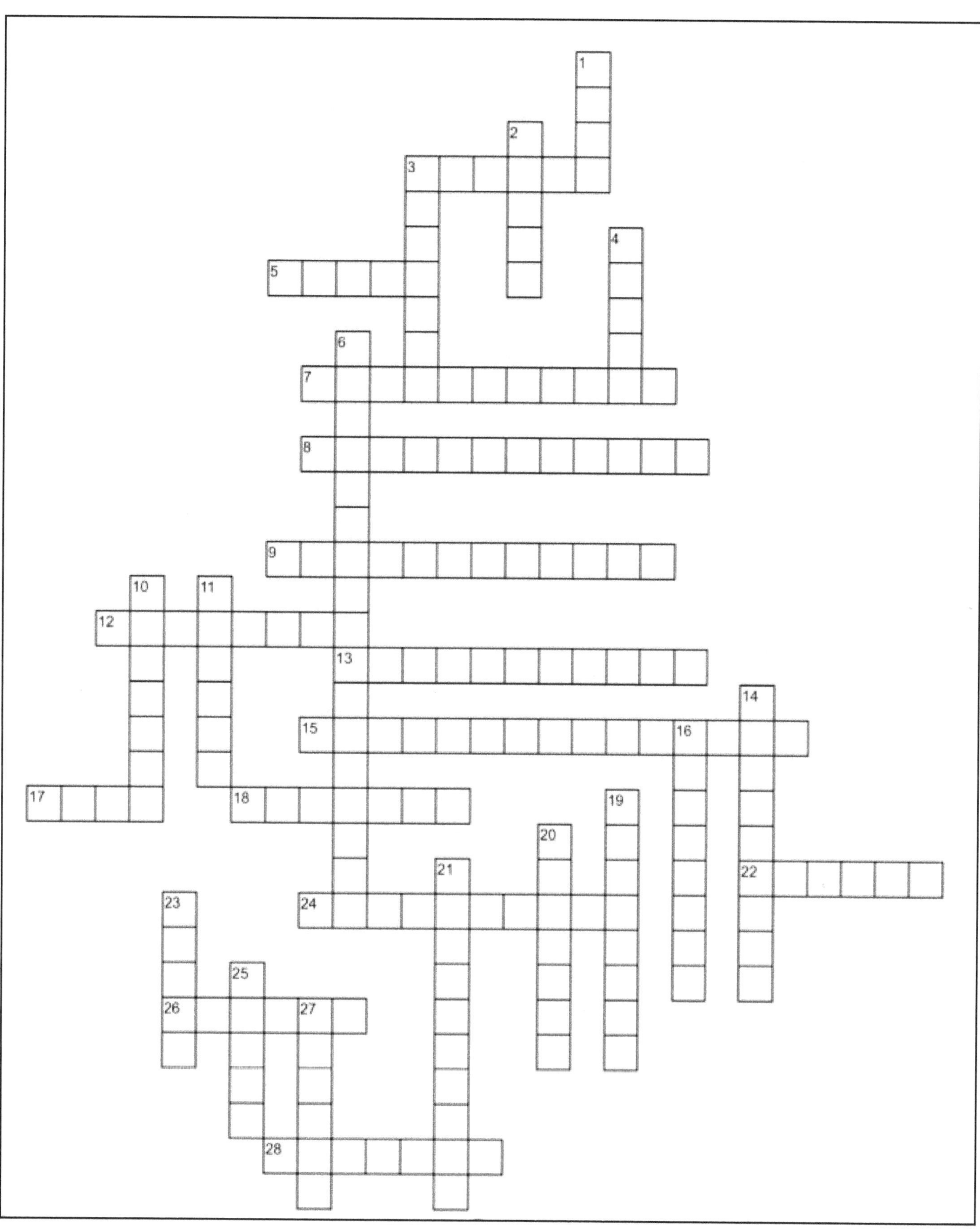

Commanders of the Civil War Word Search

H	N	E	A	R	L	Y	D	B	R	A	G	G	E
O	O	K	Y	S	A	M	O	H	T	K	G	H	P
O	S	L	N	T	S	T	N	A	R	G	B	H	P
K	K	M	O	J	U	K	S	H	E	R	M	A	N
E	C	C	U	N	O	G	N	Y	B	S	O	M	J
R	A	C	B	O	G	L	A	A	F	S	A	O	T
P	J	L	F	N	T	S	E	R	B	B	H	E	E
I	K	E	O	A	R	Q	T	E	R	N	V	D	D
C	E	L	R	D	A	R	M	R	S	A	I	C	R
K	D	L	R	I	U	Q	E	T	E	S	F	U	O
E	A	A	E	R	T	J	O	W	N	E	K	S	F
T	E	N	S	E	S	N	Y	R	E	T	T	T	U
T	M	M	T	H	M	V	U	E	W	L	E	E	B
A	J	N	G	S	B	B	H	O	O	D	L	R	O

Search for the names: up, down or diagonal.

UNION GENERALS

BANKS
BUFORD
BURNSIDE
CUSTER
GRANT
HOOKER
McCLELLAN
MEADE
SHERIDAN
SHERMAN
THOMAS

UNION ADMIRAL

FARRAGUT

CONFEDERATE GENERALS

BRAGG
EARLY
EWELL
FORREST
HOOD
JACKSON
JOHNSTON
LEE
LONGSTREET
MOSBY
PICKETT
STUART

Civil Rights Leaders Word Search

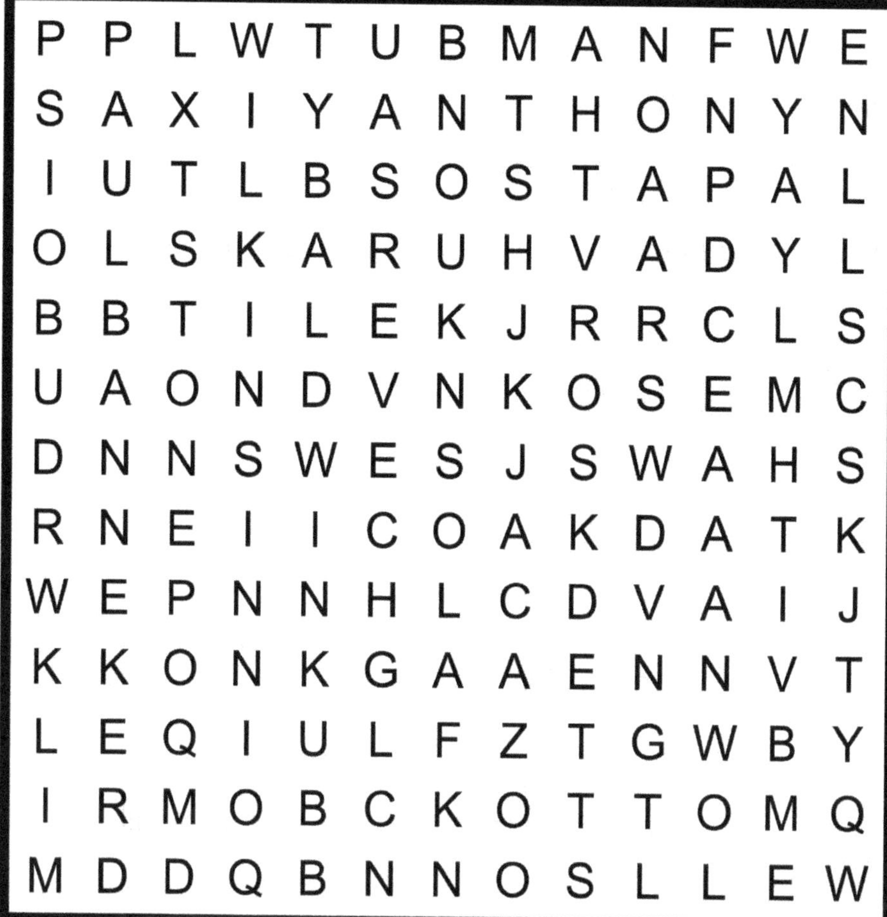
P P L W T U B M A N F W E
S A X I Y A N T H O N Y N
I U T L B S O S T A P A L
O L S K A R U H V A D Y L
B B T I L E K J R R C L S
U A O N D V N K O S E M C
D N N S W E S J S W A H S
R N E I I C O A K D A T K
W E P N N H L C D V A I J
K K O N K G A A E N N V T
L E Q I U L F Z T G W B Y
I R M O B C K O T T O M Q
M D D Q B N N O S L L E W

ABOLITIONISTS, SUFFRAGE ADVOCATES AND OTHER CIVIL RIGHTS LEADERS

Search for last names only: up, down or diagonal.

First and middle names are shown in parentheses.

ADDAMS (Jane)
ANTHONY (Susan B.)
BALDWIN (James)
BANNEKER (Benjamin)
BLACKWELL (Antoinette Brown)
CATT (Carrie Chapman)
CHAVEZ (Cesar)
DOUGLASS (Frederick)
DU BOIS (W.E.B.)
EVERS (Medgar)
INNIS (Roy)
JORDAN (Barbara)
KING (Martin Luther, Jr.)
MILK(Harvey)
MOTT (Lucretia)
PARKS (Rosa)
PAUL (Alice)
STANTON (Elizabeth Cady)
STONE (Lucy)
TUBMAN (Harriet)
WELLS (Ida B.)
WILKINS (Roy)

Hidden Cities

Find the United States city hiding in each sentence.

1. Chandal, last in line, closed the door behind her.
A city in Texas.

2. Because she was hosting the party, Tam paid the restaurant bill.
A city in Florida.

3. "Are Noah, Sam, and Jeff going to the beach with you?" Jake's mom asked.
A city in Nevada.

4. Alan cast Eric's ball over the cliff in anger.
A city in Pennsylvania.

5. Every day Tony goes to the gym with his brother.
A city in Ohio.

6. "I cannot drive you, so you will have to take a cab, Ilene," said her father.
A city in Texas.

7. John, the club's golf pro, voted to change the course from private to public.
A city in Utah.

8. Alan sings in the high school's a cappella group.
A city in Michigan.

9. Ella saw a jumbo stone crab in the sand.
A city in Massachusetts.

10. The beautiful garden very likely was her pride and joy.
A city in Colorado

Solutions*

***Optional Lists of Answers**

Alphabetical lists of the answers are provided. These may be used to help solve the puzzle from the beginning, to assist those having difficulty, or not at all.

Settlement and Colonization

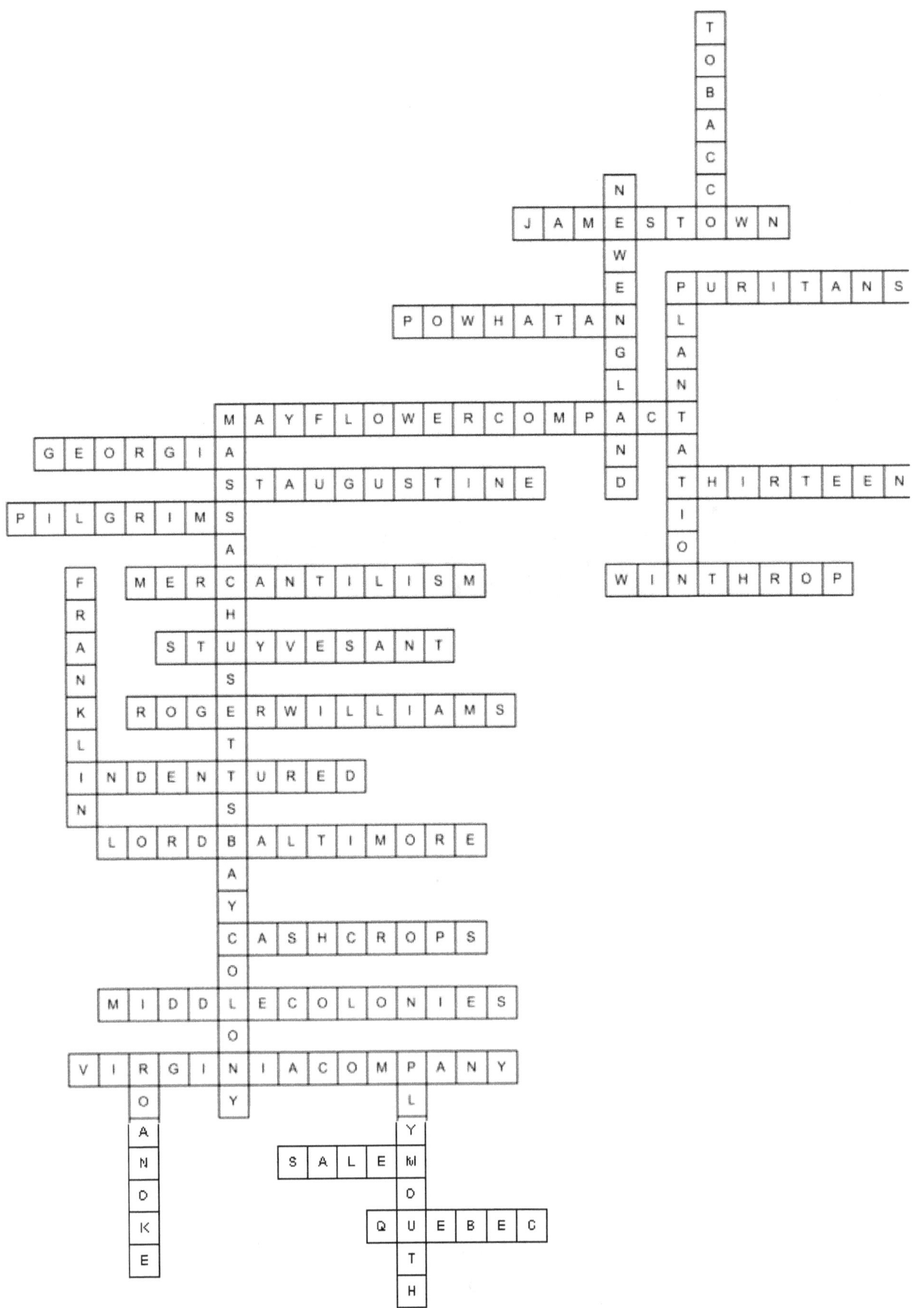

The American Revolution

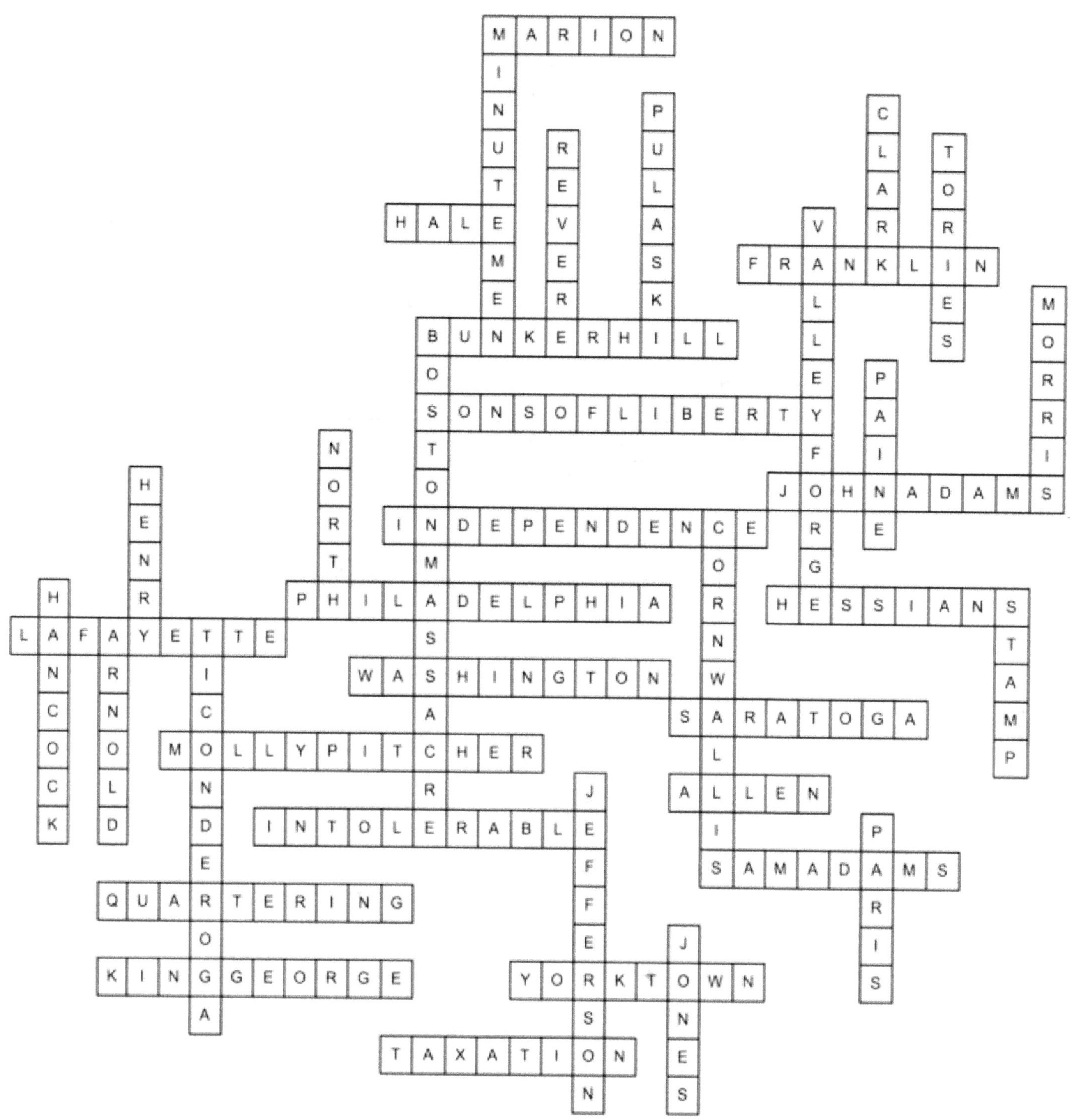

Westward Expansion

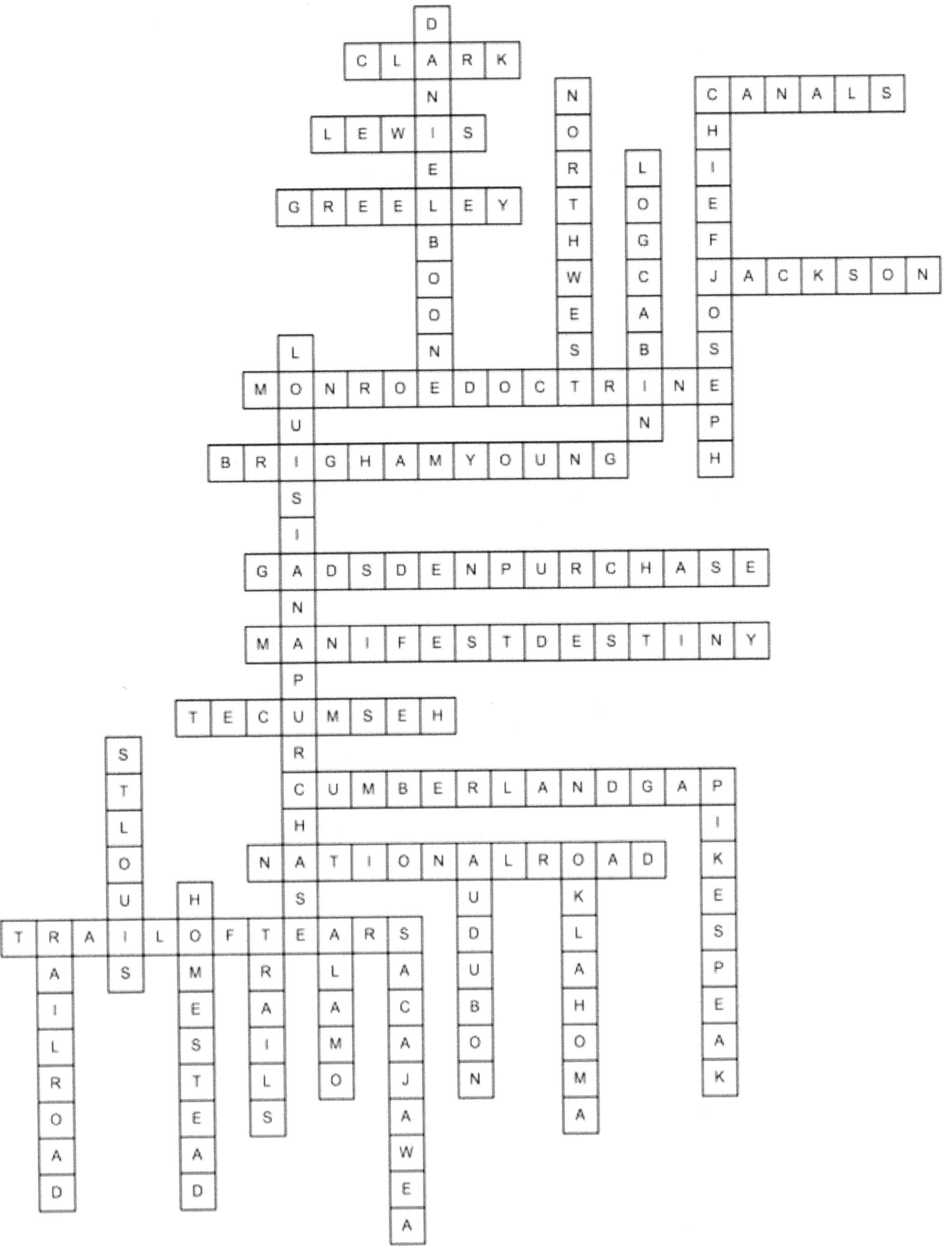

The American Civil War

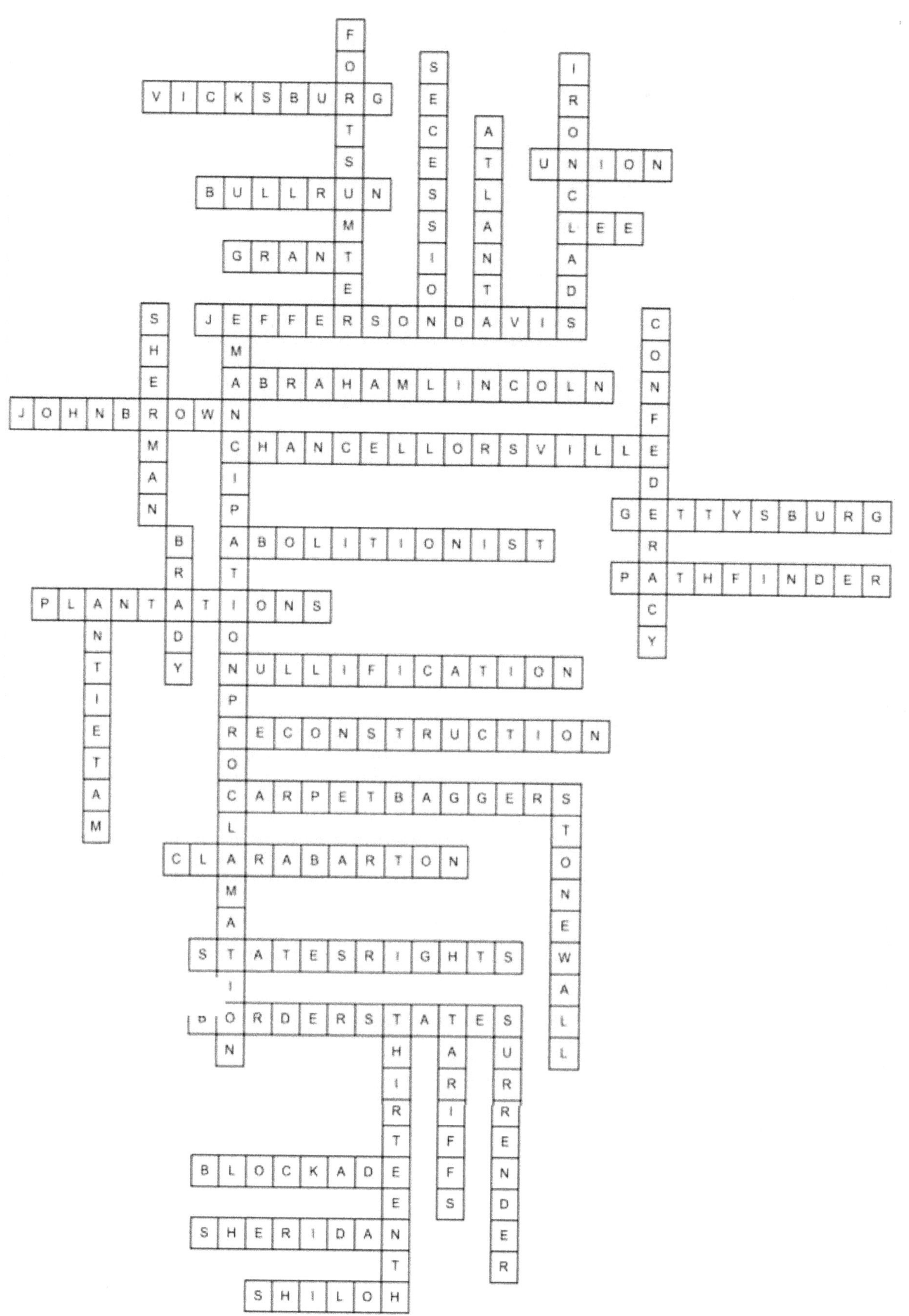

Immigration

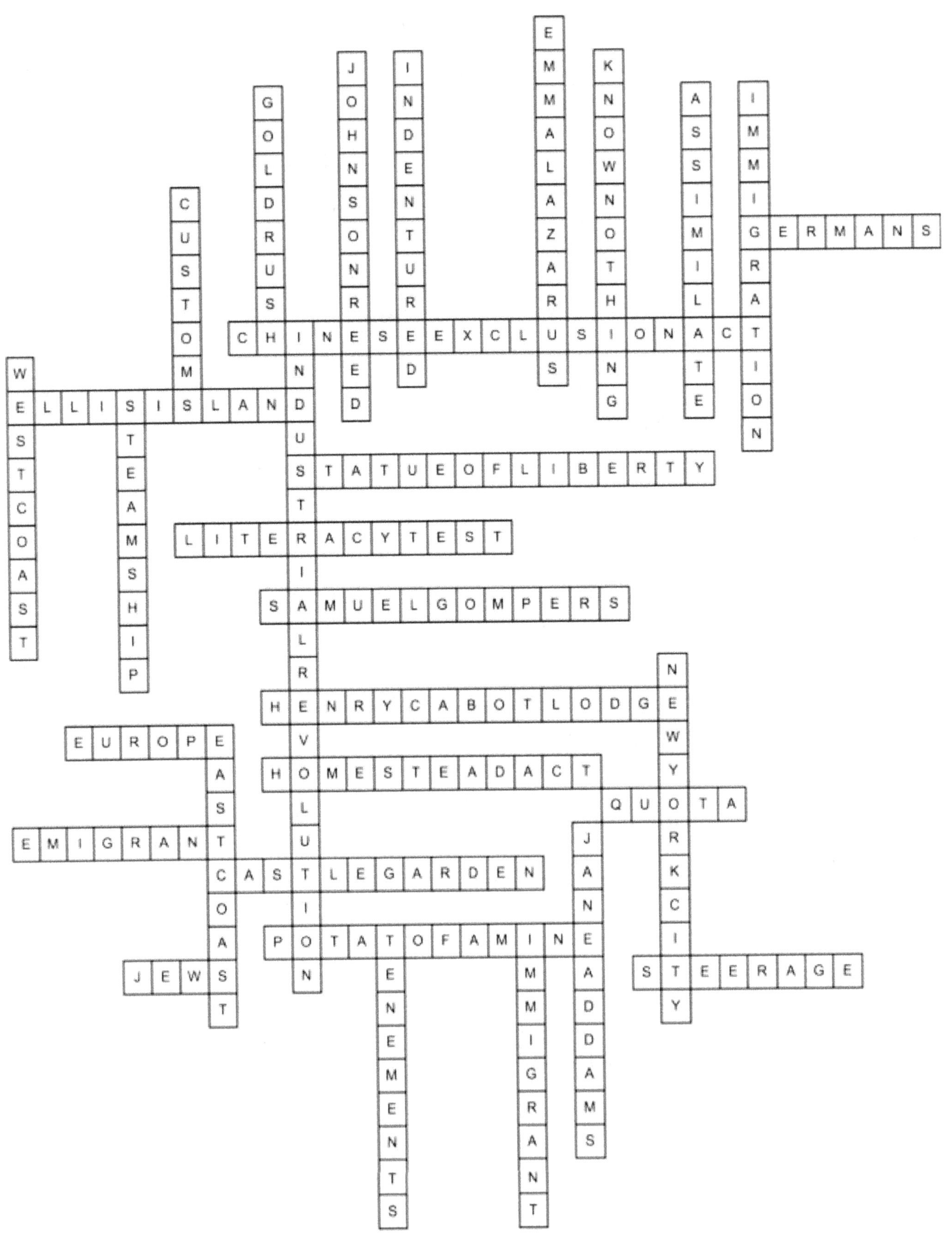

EMMALAZARUS
JOHNSONREED
INDENTURED
KNOWNOTHING
ASSIMILATE
IMMIGRATION
GOLDRUSH
CUSTOM
GERMANS
CHINESEEXCLUSIONACT
WESTCOAST
ELLISISLAND
STEAMSHIP
INDUSTRIALREVOLUTION
STATUEOFLIBERTY
LITERACYTEST
SAMUELGOMPERS
NEWYORKCITY
HENRYCABOTLODGE
EUROPE
EASTCOAST
HOMESTEADACT
QUOTA
JANEADDAMS
EMIGRANT
CASTLEGARDEN
POTATOFAMINE
JEWS
STEERAGE
TENEMENTS
IMMIGRANT

Industrial Revolution

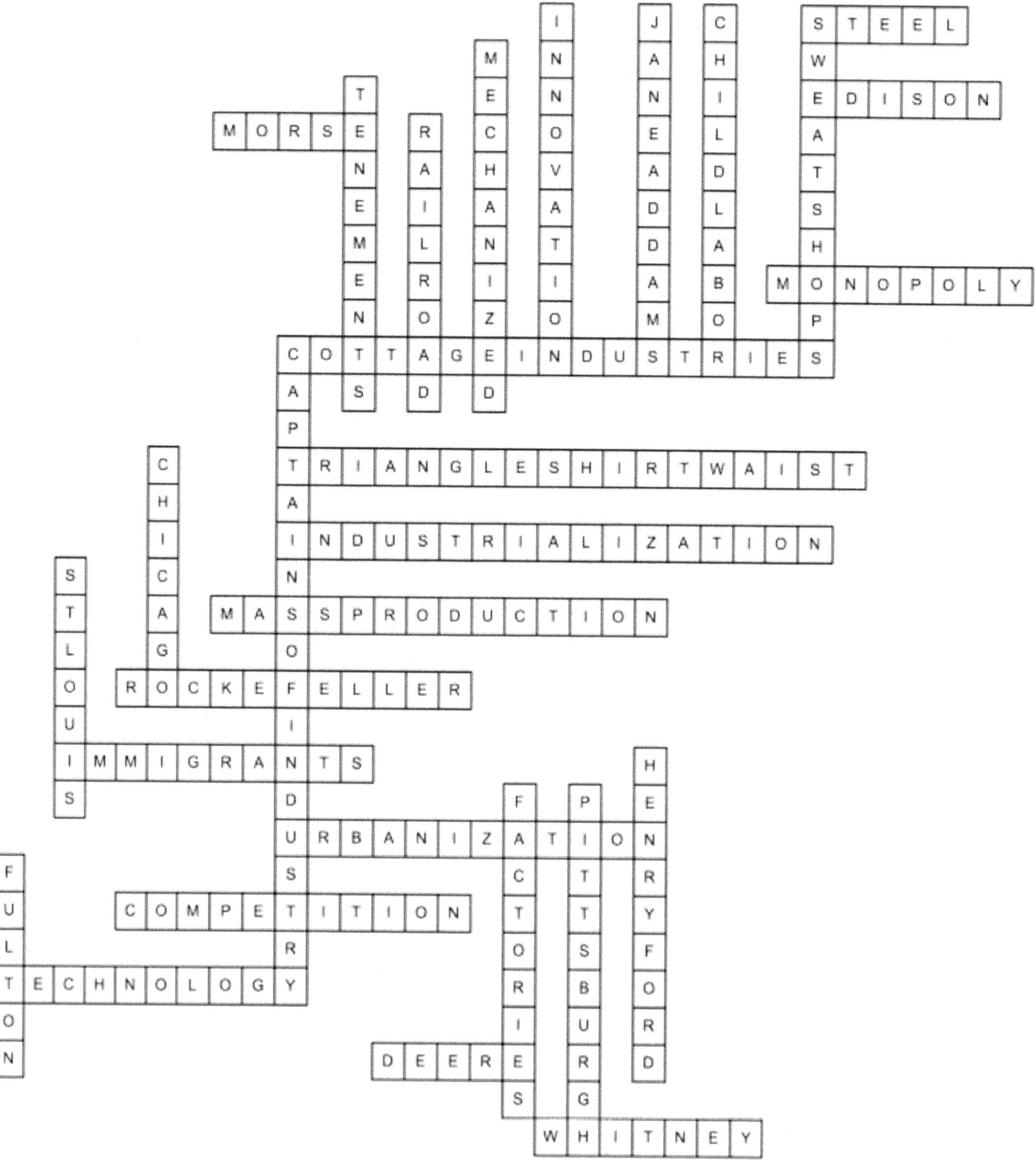

Presidents of the United States

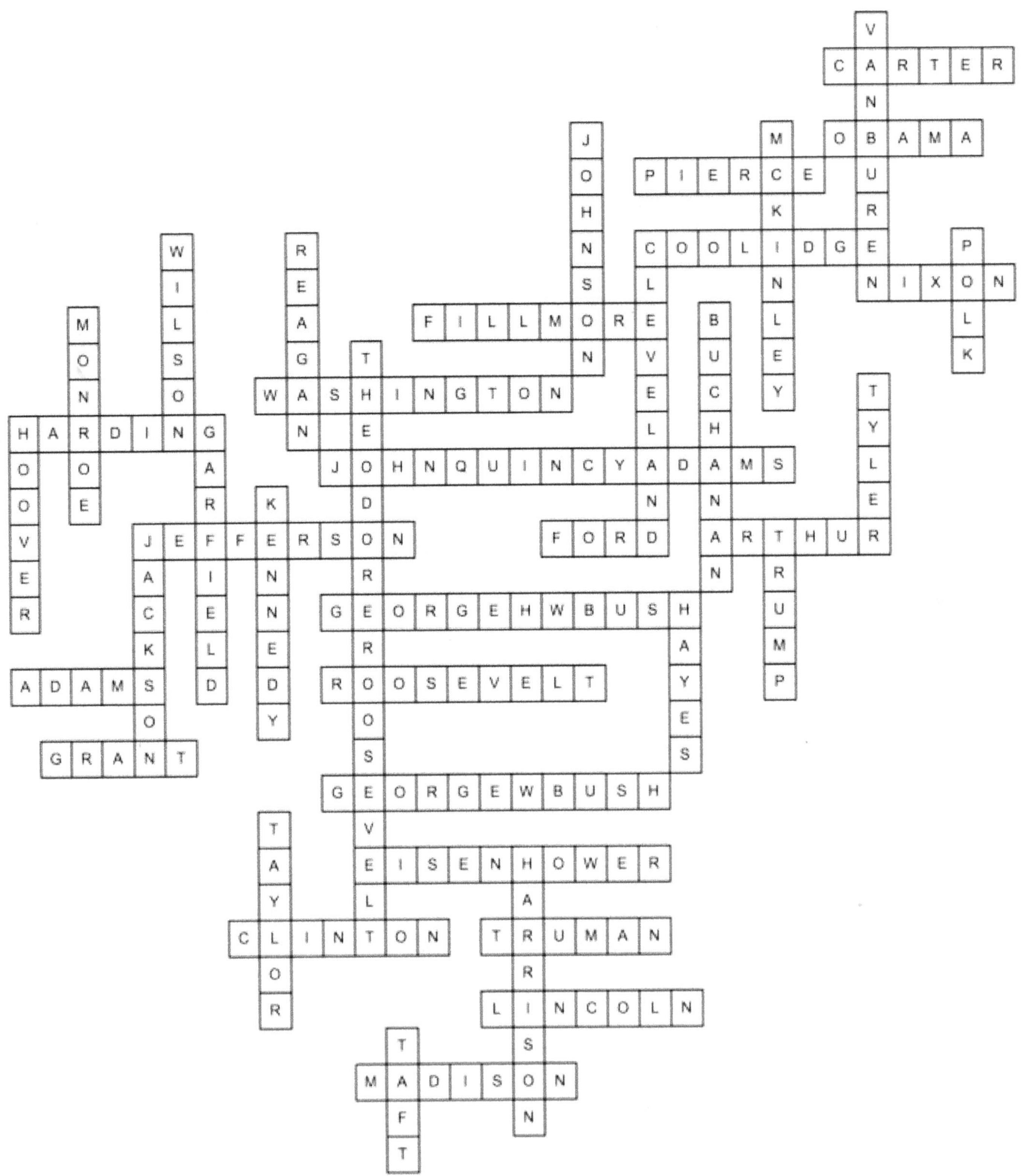

Civics and Government

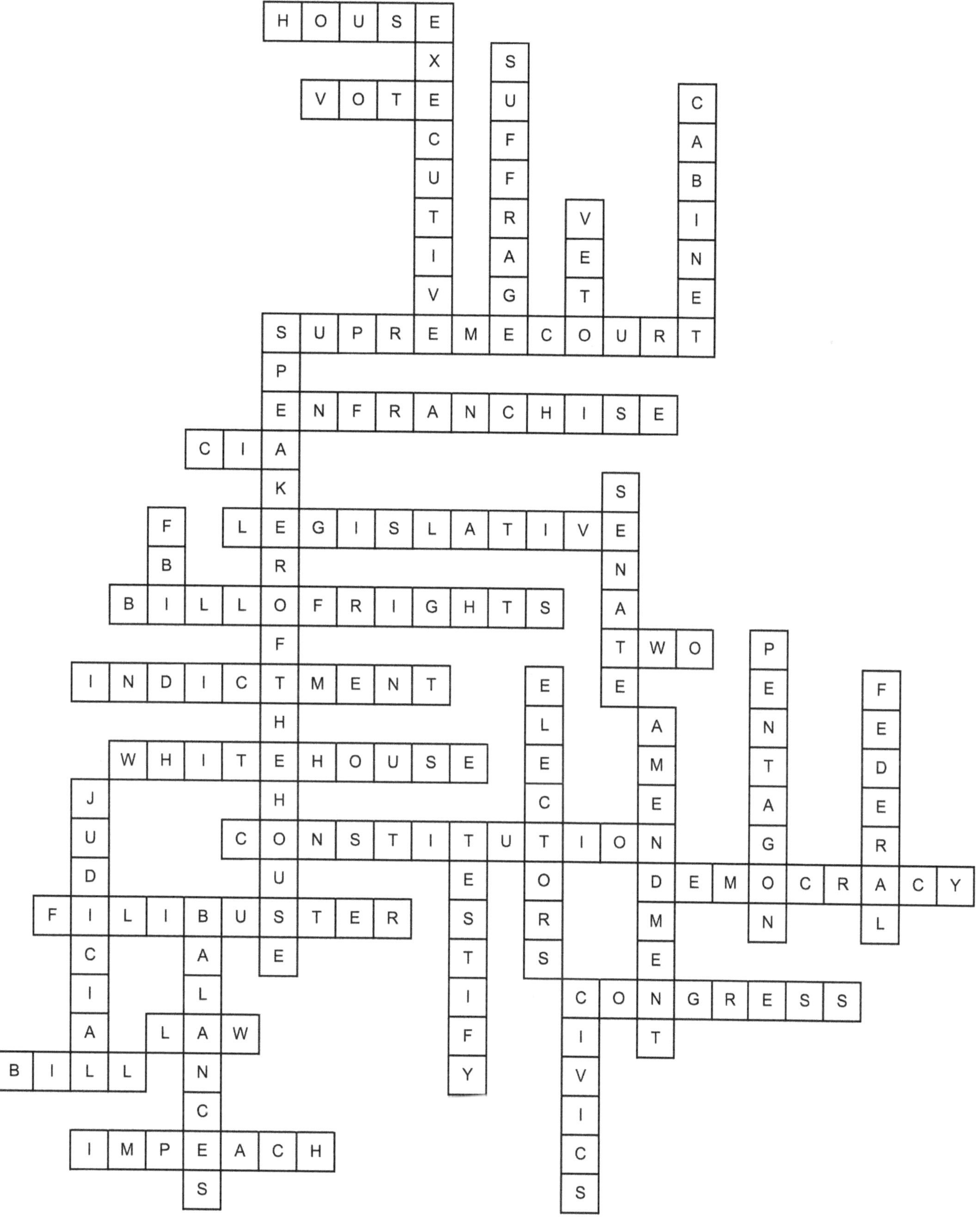

Civil Rights

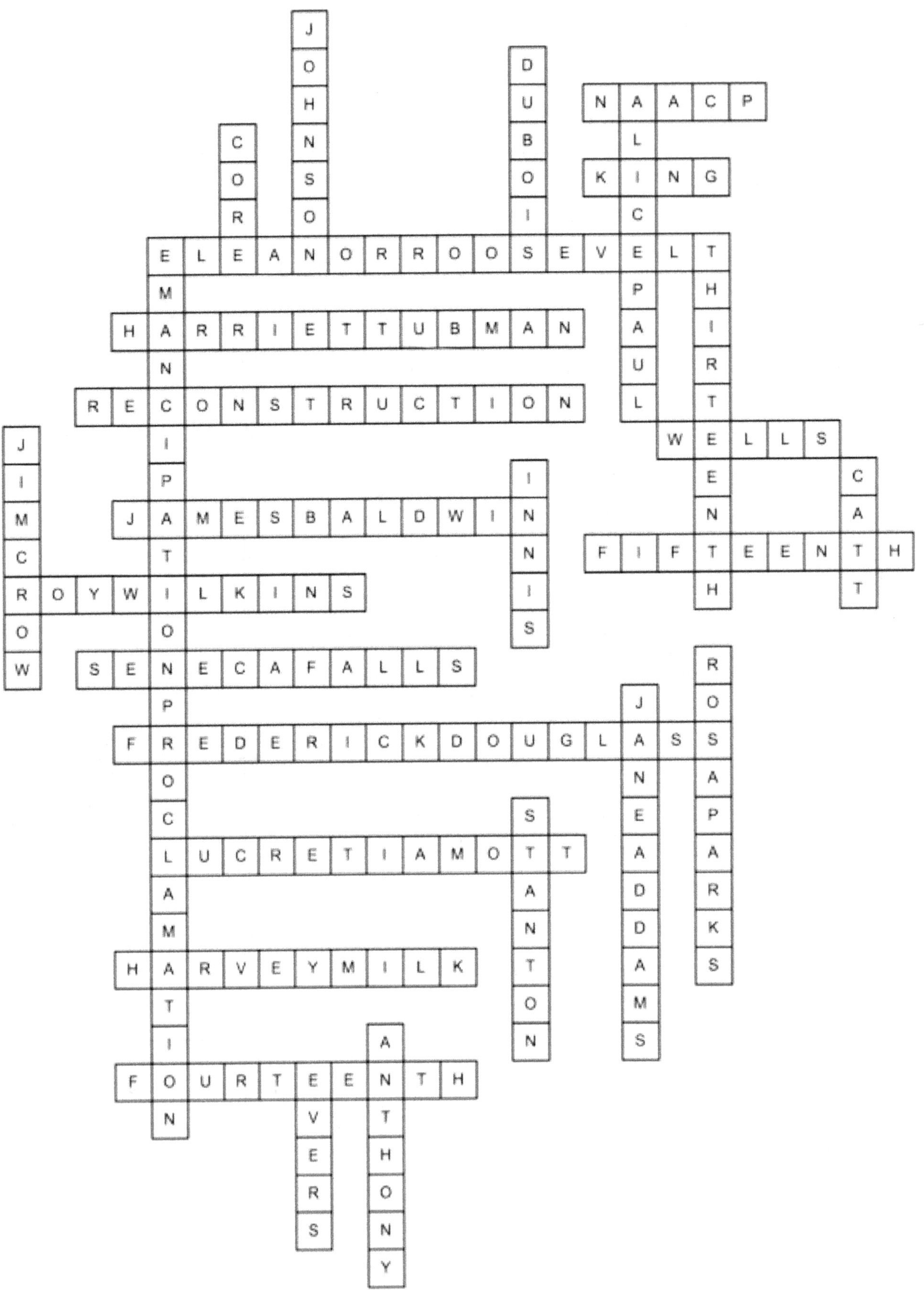

U.S. History Potpourri

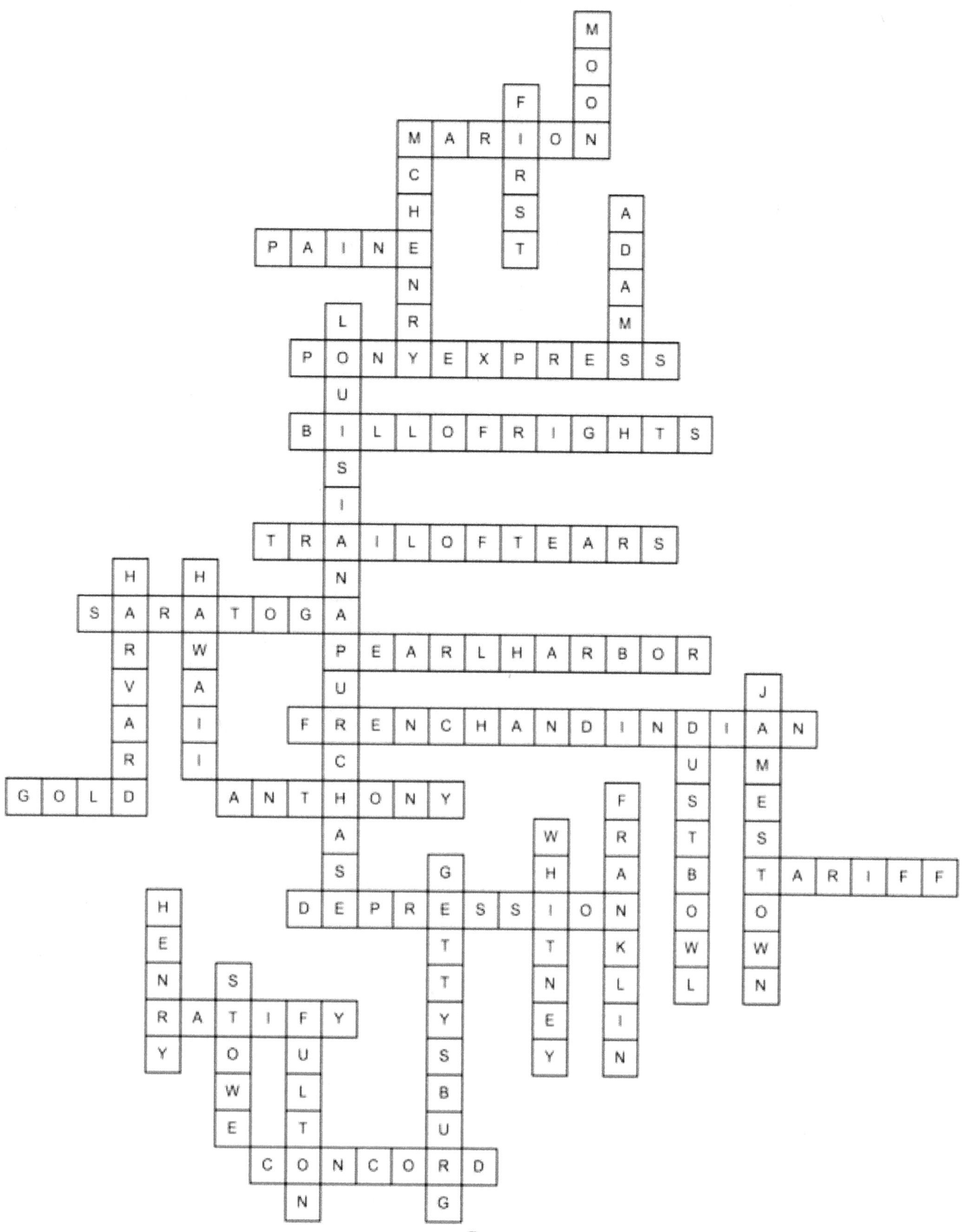

Commanders of the Civil War Word Search

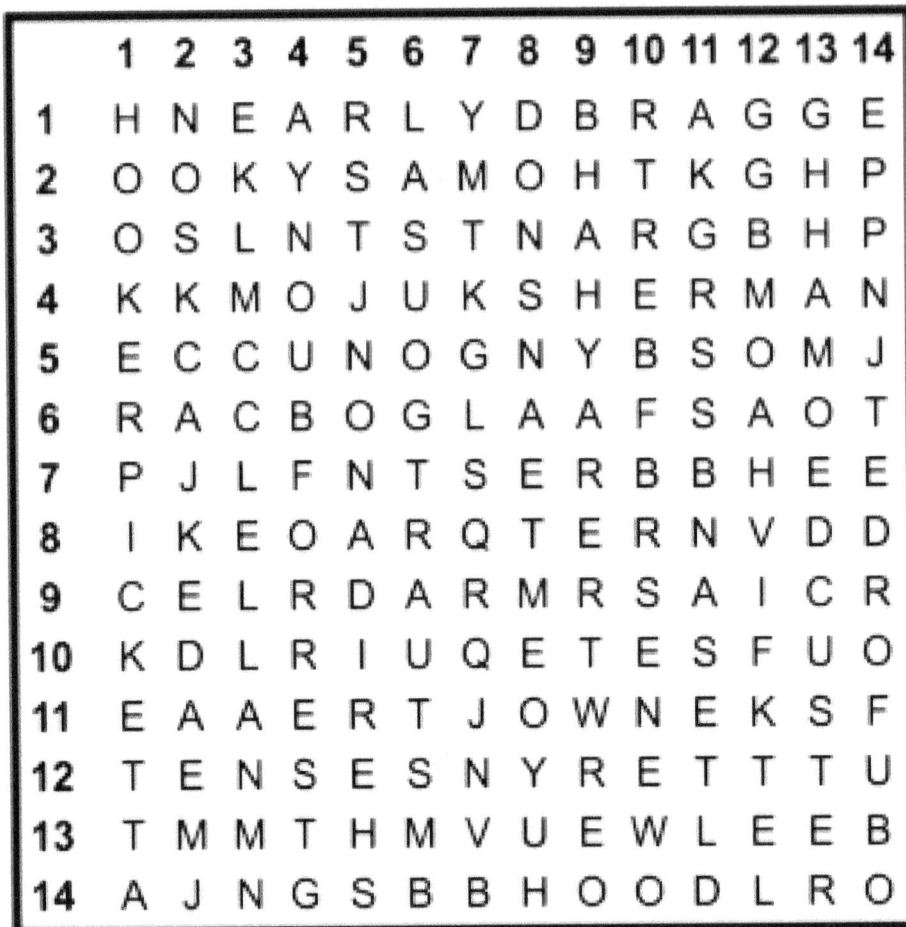

	1	2	3	4	5	6	7	8	9	10	11	12	13	14
1	H	N	E	A	R	L	Y	D	B	R	A	G	G	E
2	O	O	K	Y	S	A	M	O	H	T	K	G	H	P
3	O	S	L	N	T	S	T	N	A	R	G	B	H	P
4	K	K	M	O	J	U	K	S	H	E	R	M	A	N
5	E	C	C	U	N	O	G	N	Y	B	S	O	M	J
6	R	A	C	B	O	G	L	A	A	F	S	A	O	T
7	P	J	L	F	N	T	S	E	R	B	B	H	E	E
8	I	K	E	O	A	R	Q	T	E	R	N	V	D	D
9	C	E	L	R	D	A	R	M	R	S	A	I	C	R
10	K	D	L	R	I	U	Q	E	T	E	S	F	U	O
11	E	A	A	E	R	T	J	O	W	N	E	K	S	F
12	T	E	N	S	E	S	N	Y	R	E	T	T	T	U
13	T	M	M	T	H	M	V	U	E	W	L	E	E	B
14	A	J	N	G	S	B	B	H	O	O	D	L	R	O

The names below are listed with their starting row and column.

UNION GENERALS

BANKS 7:10
BUFORD 13:14
BURNSIDE 14:7
CUSTER 9:13
GRANT 3:11
HOOKER 1:1
McCLELLAN 4:3
MEADE 13:2
SHERIDAN 14:5
SHERMAN 4:8
THOMAS 2:10

UNION ADMIRAL

FARRAGUT 10:12

CONFEDERATE GENERALS

BRAGG 1:9
EARLY 1:3
EWELL 10:8
FORREST 7:4
HOOD 14:8
JACKSON 7:2
JOHNSTON 5:14
LEE 6:7
LONGSTREET 3:3
MOSBY 5:13
PICKETT 7:1
STUART12:6

Civil Rights Leaders Word Search

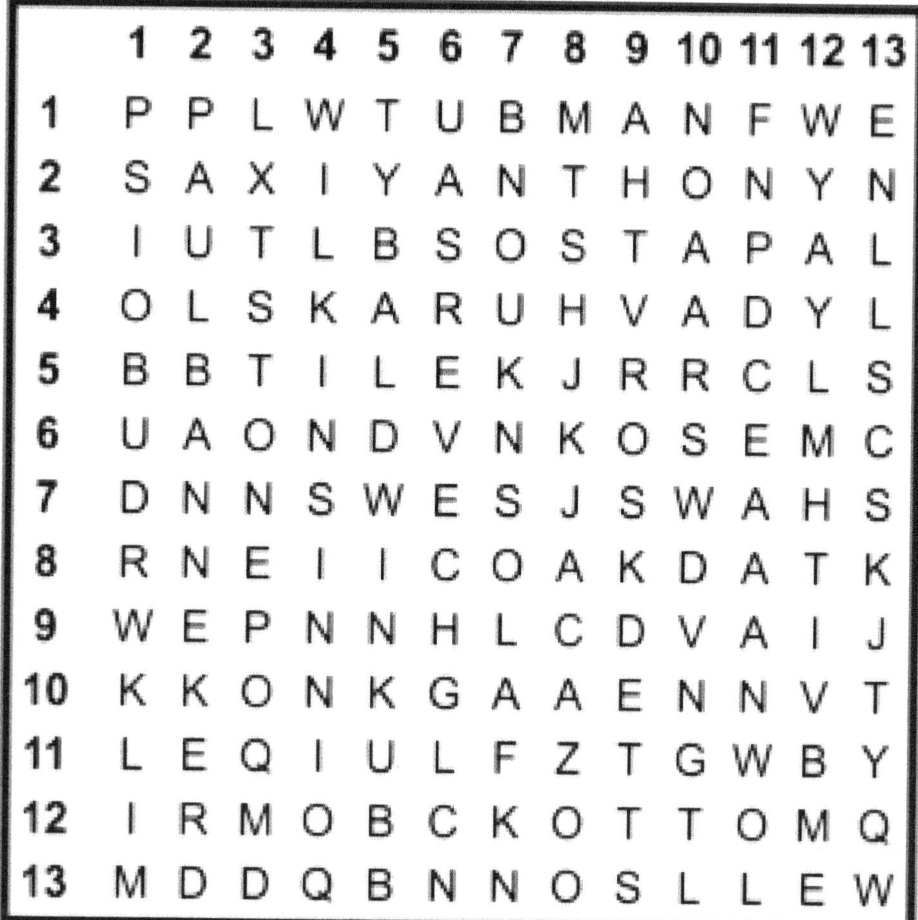

	1	2	3	4	5	6	7	8	9	10	11	12	13
1	P	P	L	W	T	U	B	M	A	N	F	W	E
2	S	A	X	I	Y	A	N	T	H	O	N	Y	N
3	I	U	T	L	B	S	O	S	T	A	P	A	L
4	O	L	S	K	A	R	U	H	V	A	D	Y	L
5	B	B	T	I	L	E	K	J	R	R	C	L	S
6	U	A	O	N	D	V	N	K	O	S	E	M	C
7	D	N	N	S	W	E	S	J	S	W	A	H	S
8	R	N	E	I	I	C	O	A	K	D	A	T	K
9	W	E	P	N	N	H	L	C	D	V	A	I	J
10	K	K	O	N	K	G	A	A	E	N	N	V	T
11	L	E	Q	I	U	L	F	Z	T	G	W	B	Y
12	I	R	M	O	B	C	K	O	T	T	O	M	Q
13	M	D	D	Q	B	N	N	O	S	L	L	E	W

ABOLITIONISTS, SUFFRAGE ADVOCATES AND OTHER CIVIL RIGHTS LEADERS
The names below are listed with their starting row and column.

ADDAMS (Jane) 10:8
ANTHONY (Susan B.) 2:6
BALDWIN (James) 3:5
BANNEKER (Benjamin) 5:2
BLACKWELL (Antoinette Brown) 12:5
CATT (Carrie Chapman) 5:11
CHAVEZ (Cesar) 6:13
DOUGLASS (Frederick) 13:3
DU BOIS (W.E.B.) 7:1
EVERS (Medgar) 7:6
INNIS (Roy) 11:4
JORDAN (Barbara) 7:8
KING (Martin Luther, Jr.) 8:13
MILK (Harvey) 13:1
MOTT (Lucretia) 12:12
PARKS (Rosa) 3:11
PAUL (Alice) 1:2
STANTON (Elizabeth Cady) 7:13
STONE (Lucy) 4:3
TUBMAN (Harriet) 1:5
WELLS (Ida B.) 13:13
WILKINS (Roy) 1:4

Hidden Cities

The city in each sentence is in bold.

1. Chan**dal, las**t in line, closed the door behind her.
A city in Texas.

2. Because she was hosting the party, **Tam pa**id the restaurant bill.
A city in Florida.

3. "A**re No**ah, Sam, and Jeff going to the beach with you?" Jake's mom asked.
A city in Nevada.

4. A**lan cast Er**ic's ball over the cliff in anger.
A city in Pennsylvania.

5. Every **day Ton**y goes to the gym with his brother.
A city in Ohio.

6. "I cannot drive you, so you will have to take a c**ab, Ilene**," said her father.
A city in Texas.

7. John, the club's golf **pro, vo**ted to change the course from private to public.
A city in Utah.

8. A**lan sing**s in the high school's a cappella group.
A city in Michigan.

9. Ella saw a jum**bo ston**e crab in the sand.
A city in Massachusetts.

10. The beautiful gar**den ver**y likely was her pride and joy.
A city in Colorado

Optional Lists of Words and Terms

These lists are provided for your convenience. If a puzzle is used as an introduction or just for fun, you might want to provide the list of words. On the other hand, if the puzzle is being done in lieu of a quiz, you might choose not to utilize them. In either case, solutions to the puzzles are provided.

Settlement and Colonization

cash crops Franklin Georgia indentured Jamestown Lord Baltimore Massachusetts Bay Colony Mayflower Compact mercantilism Middle Colonies New England Stuyvesant Pilgrims plantation Plymouth Powhatan Puritans Quebec Roanoke Roger Williams Salem St. Augustine thirteen tobacco Virginia Company Winthrop

The American Revolution

John Adams Sam Adams Allen Arnold Boston Massacre Bunker Hill Clark Cornwallis Hancock Independence Franklin Hale Henry Hessians Intolerable Acts Jefferson Jones King George Lafayette Minutemen Marion Molly Pitcher Morris North Paine Philadelphia Pulaski Quartering Paris Revere Saratoga Sons of Liberty Stamp Ticonderoga Tories Valley Forge Washington Yorktown Taxation

Westward Expansion

Alamo Audubon Brigham Young canals Chief Joseph Clark Cumberland Gap Daniel Boone Gadsden Purchase Greeley Homestead Jackson Lewis log cabin Louisiana Purchase Manifest Destiny Monroe Doctrine National Road Northwest Oklahoma Pikes Peak railroad Sacajawea St. Louis Tecumseh Trail of Tears Trails

The American Civil War

abolitionist Abraham Lincoln Antietam Atlanta blockade border states Brady Bull Run Carpetbaggers Chancellorsville Clara Barton Confederacy Emancipation Proclamation Fort Sumter Gettysburg Grant ironclads Jefferson Davis John Brown Lee nullification Pathfinder plantations Reconstruction secession Sheridan Sherman Shiloh states' rights Stonewall surrender tariffs thirteenth Union Vicksburg

Immigration

assimilate Castle Garden Chinese Exclusion Act Customs East Coast Ellis Island emigrant Emma Lazarus Europe Germans gold rush Henry Cabot Lodge Homestead Act immigrant immigration Industrial Revolution indentured Jane Addams Jews Johnson-Reed Know-Nothing literacy test New York City potato famine quota Samuel Gompers Statue of Liberty steamship steerage tenements West Coast

The Industrial Revolution

captains of industry Chicago child labor competition cottage industries Deere Edison factories Henry Ford Fulton immigrants industrialization innovation Jane Addams Morse Rockefeller mass production mechanized monopoly Pittsburgh Railroad St. Louis steel sweatshops technology tenements Triangle Shirtwaist Company Urbanization Whitney

U.S. Presidents & Dates Served

1. George Washington (1789–1797)
2. John Adams (1797–1801)
3. Thomas Jefferson (1801–1809)
4. James Madison (1809–1817)
5. James Monroe (1817–1825)
6. John Quincy Adams (1825–1829)
7. Andrew Jackson (1829–1837)
8. Martin Van Buren (1837–1841)
9. William Henry Harrison (1841)
10. John Tyler (1841–1845)
11. James K. Polk (1845–1849)
12. Zachary Taylor (1849–1850)
13. Millard Fillmore (1850–1853)
14. Franklin Pierce (1853–1857)
15. James Buchanan (1857–1861)
16. Abraham Lincoln (1861–1865)
17. Andrew Johnson (1865–1869)
18. Ulysses S. Grant (1869–1877)
19. Rutherford B. Hayes (1877–1881)
20. James A. Garfield (1881)
21. Chester Arthur (1881–1885)
22. Grover Cleveland (1885–1889)
23. Benjamin Harrison (1889–1893)
24. Grover Cleveland (1893–1897)
25. William McKinley (1897–1901)
26. Theodore Roosevelt (1901–1909)
27. William Howard Taft (1909–1913)
28. Woodrow Wilson (1913–1921)
29. Warren G. Harding (1921–1923)
30. Calvin Coolidge (1923–1929)
31. Herbert Hoover (1929–1933)
32. Franklin D. Roosevelt (1933–1945)
33. Harry S. Truman (1945–1953)
34. Dwight D. Eisenhower (1953–1961)
35. John F. Kennedy (1961–1963)
36. Lyndon B. Johnson (1963–1969)
37. Richard Nixon (1969–1974)
38. Gerald Ford (1974–1977)
39. Jimmy Carter (1977–1981)
40. Ronald Reagan (1981–1989)
41. George Bush (1989–1993)
42. Bill Clinton (1993–2001)
43. George W. Bush (2001–2009)
44. Barack Obama (2009–2017)
45. Donald Trump (2017–)

Immigration

assimilate   Castle Garden   Chinese Exclusion Act
Customs   East Coast   Ellis Island   emigrant
Emma Lazarus   Europe   Germans   gold rush
Henry Cabot Lodge   Homestead Act   immigrant
immigration   Industrial Revolution   indentured
Jane Addams   Jews   Johnson-Reed   Know-Nothing
literacy test   New York City   potato famine   quota
Samuel Gompers   Statue of Liberty   steamship
steerage   tenements   West Coast

Civics and Government

amendment   balances   bill   Bill of Rights   Cabinet
CIA   civics   Congress   Constitution   democracy
electors   enfranchise   Executive   FBI   federal
filibuster   House   impeach   indictment   Judicial
law   Legislative   Pentagon   Senate
Speaker of the House   suffrage   Supreme Court
testify   two   veto   vote   White House

Civil Rights: Whole names are given here, but follow instructions for each clue.

Jane Addams   Susan B. Anthony   James Baldwin
Carrie Chapman Catt   CORE   Frederick Douglass
W.E.B. Du Bois   Emancipation Proclamation
Medgar Evers   fifteenth   fourteenth   Harvey Milk
Roy Innis   Jim Crow   Lyndon Baines Johnson
Martin Luther King, Jr.   Lucretia Mott   Reconstruction
Rosa Parks   Eleanor Roosevelt   NAACP   Alice Paul
Seneca Falls   Elizabeth Cady Stanton   thirteenth
Harriet Tubman   Ida Wells   Roy Wilkins

U.S. History Potpourri

Adams   Anthony   Bill of Rights   Concord
Depression   Dust Bowl   first   Franklin
French and Indian   Fulton   Gettysburg   gold
Harvard   Hawaii   Henry   Jamestown
Louisiana Purchase   Marion   McHenry   moon
Paine   Pearl Harbor   Pony Express   ratify
Saratoga   Stowe   tariff   Trail of Tears   Whitney